UNIVERSITY OF STRATHCLYDE

30125 00420374 0

26594196

KV-038-656

Department of the Environment

Planning, Pollution and Waste Management

Books to

D
628.54
PL17

Environmental Resources Limited

in association with

Oxford Polytechnic School of Planning

ANDERSONIAN LIBRARY
★
WITHDRAWN
FROM
LIBRARY
STOCK
★
UNIVERSITY OF STRATHCLYDE

London: HMSO

14 SEP 1992

© Crown copyright 1992

Applications for reproduction should be made to HMSO

First published 1992

ISBN 0 11 752668 1

Recycled Paper

Cover photograph: High Temperature Incinerator at Ellesmere Port. Cleanaway Limited

The findings and recommendations presented in this report represent the views of Environmental Resources Limited and Oxford Polytechnic School of Planning. They do not necessarily represent the views of the Secretary of State or of any organisations consulted during the research.

ERL April 1992

This report has been prepared by Environmental Resources Limited with all reasonable skill, care and diligence within the Terms of Contract with the Client incorporating Environmental Resources Limited's General Terms and Conditions of Business.

ERL will accept no liability of whatsoever nature for claims from third parties to whom the contents of this report are made known directly or indirectly by the Client.

ERL April 1992

CONTENTS

EXECUTIVE SUMMARY

In December 1991 the Department of the Environment commissioned ERL, together with the Oxford Polytechnic School of Planning, to carry out a research project on the relationship between planning controls and pollution and waste management controls. This report presents the findings of that research which comprised :

- a review of published literature;
- interviews with about 20 local authorities;
- interviews with the pollution control agencies and other interested organisations;
- reviews of about 30 development plans and about 40 development control case studies.

The project has been guided by a Steering Group comprising representatives of interested sections of the Department, and of the pollution control agencies, local government and the legal profession.

The aim of the research was to assist the Department in drafting a Planning Policy Guidance Note on Planning, Pollution and Waste. On the basis of our research we have therefore developed recommendations on matters which should be covered in the proposed PPG. These can be summarised as follows:

- The PPG should provide for planning authorities, an explanation of the pollution control regimes, describing the scope of their powers and the authorisation and consent procedures they operate. The aim of this part of the PPG would be to overcome the lack of confidence in the pollution control regimes evidenced in local planning authorities, which arises very largely from the past history of pollution control in this country.

- The PPG should advise local planning authorities to consult extensively on applications for potentially polluting development. It should also provide guidance to all parties on facilitating the consultation process through understanding the needs and capabilities of all sides and by encouraging the establishment of closer links between the organisations involved.

- The PPG should advise planning authorities, and through them the other agencies and developers, on the scope of material considerations regarding pollution, on the assessment of pollution risks and on the use of conditions to limit the risk of pollution affecting the use of land.

- The PPG should also:

  - advise against the acceptance of outline applications for potentially polluting development;

  - advise planning authorities to seek information from applicants on other authorisations that will be required;

- encourage planning authorities to comment on matters of concern to planning during consultation on applications for pollution control authorisation.

- Finally the PPG :

- should treat planning and pollution separately from planning and waste management as the two topics raise fundamentally different sets of issues;

- should be addressed to the pollution control agencies and developers as well as to planning authorities and;

- should be as concise as possible.

ABBREVIATIONS

BAT	Best Available Techniques
BATNEEC	Best Available Techniques Not Entailing Excessive Cost
BPEO	Best Practicable Environmental Option
BPM	Best Practicable Means
COPA 1974	Control of Pollution Act 1974
EA	Environmental Assessment
EPA 1990	Environmental Protection Act 1990
EQO	Environmental Quality Objectives
ES	Environmental Statement
HMIP	Her Majesty's Inspectorate of Pollution
HMIPI	Her Majesty's Industrial Pollution Inspectorate (in Scotland)
HSE	Health & Safety Executive
IPC	Integrated Pollution Control
LAAPC	Local Authority Air Pollution Control
LPA	Local Planning Authority
MPG	Minerals Planning Guidance
NRA	National Rivers Authority
PPG	Planning Policy Guidance
RPG	Regional Planning Guidance
WDDP	Waste Disposal Development Plan (or Waste Local Plan)
WDP	Waste Disposal Plan
WLP	See WDDP
WRA	Waste Regulation Authority
WRA 1991	Water Resources Act 1991

1.1   *OBJECTIVES*

This document is the final report of a study commissioned by the
Department of the Environment on:

- *the relationship between planning controls and pollution and waste management controls.*

The study was undertaken by Environmental Resources Limited in
association with the Oxford Polytechnic School of Planning.

In the 1990 White Paper "*This Common Inheritance*" the government undertook
to '*consider the need for ... guidance on the relationship between planning and
pollution control in the light of new measures in the Environmental Protection Bill'*.
The objective of the study is to provide information to assist the Department
in the preparation of that guidance, to be issued in the form of a Planning
Policy Guidance Note (PPG). The questions the research was designed to
address were as follows.

- How have local planning authorities (LPAs) taken pollution and waste
  disposal into account in determining planning applications?

- How has Environmental Assessment been used to inform the planning
  system?

- To what extent have LPAs used planning conditions and agreements to
  control pollution and waste matters?

- How are consultations with pollution control and waste control
  authorities and with other advisory bodies used as part of the
  development control process?

- How far have LPAs taken account of pollution and waste management
  issues in their development plans, including any policies for siting bad
  neighbour developments and vice versa, and to what extent have the
  relevant waste disposal plans been considered in drawing up development
  plans?

This report presents the results of the study, together with recommendations
on the content of national planning policy guidance on pollution and waste
management considerations in planning.

The planning system falls into two main parts, **development planning** and **development control**. The research has addressed treatment of pollution in both aspects of the system.

- **Development planning**: the research considers both structure and local plans, plus reference to regional and national planning guidance on which these are based. It also considers the role of and relationship to Waste Disposal Plans and the new Waste Disposal Development Plans (also known as Waste Local Plans).

- **Development control**: the research has addressed all forms of development which come within the scope of the Town and Country Planning Acts, with the exception of minerals developments which are the subject of separate guidance in Minerals Planning Guidance (MPG's). We have not specifically considered developments which receive deemed planning consent through other legislation, such as the Electricity and Pipelines Acts.

We have defined **pollution control and waste management** for the purposes of our research primarily in the terms of the Environmental Protection Act 1990 (EPA 1990). Parts I and II of the Act control pollution by substances released to air, water and land, through an authorisation regime applied to certain types of industrial activity and a licensing regime applied to waste management operations. The research has focused on the planning of developments of these types and on how the planning system deals with potential pollution of air, water and land arising from them. We have also included pollution considerations regulated by Part III of the Water Resources Act 1991 (WRA 1991) as this controls discharges to the aquatic environment from activities not regulated under EPA 1990 Part I.

As a consequence of this definition the pollution control agencies with which this study is principally concerned are: Her Majesty's Inspectorate of Pollution (HMIP), the National Rivers Authority (NRA), Local Authority Air Pollution Control Authorities (LAAPC), and local Waste Regulation Authorities (WRA).

A number of environmental protection matters have not been considered in our research, principally because they are addressed in other planning guidance. These include noise, major hazards, nature conservation, heritage and landscape. We have also not addressed the indirect pollution consequences of development such as might arise, for example, from increases in road traffic stimulated by new development [1].

The focus of our research has therefore been on new developments requiring planning permission which have the potential to cause pollution by release of substances to air, water and land. The types of development with which

---

[1] Reference has been made to noise and major hazards where there are parallels to be drawn but it is not intended that the PPG should deal centrally with these matters.

we have principally been concerned are industry and waste treatment and disposal.

1.3 APPROACH TO THE RESEARCH

The research on which this report is based was carried out between December 1991 and February 1992. It comprised five principal activities.

(i) *Review of relevant published literature.* Three main types of literature were reviewed: firstly published articles and reports (searches were carried out of relevant journals over the past 2 years); published planning guidance (circulars, PPG, MPGs, RPGs); and published and internal guidance documents on the pollution control regimes. A list of sources and key references identified is given in *Annex D.*

(ii) *Interviews with local authorities including county, district and unitary bodies*: a list of the authorities interviewed is given in *Annex D.* The authorities interviewed were selected to be representative of the range of different types of authority found in England and Wales, taking account of status, location in DoE regions, geographical location, urban-rural character and apparent experience of pollution issues. The issues explored in these interviews are identified in the interview protocol presented in *Annex D,* and the results are incorporated in the findings presented in *Annexes B* and *C.*

(iii) *Reviews of development plans*: a selection of structure, unitary and local development plans was reviewed to determine their treatment of pollution and waste issues - the policies included and the rationale for their adoption - and to establish what reference was made in them to waste and Waste Disposal Plans. Any policies on consultation with pollution control agencies were also identified. The development plans reviewed are listed in *Annex D* and the results of the review are presented in *Annex B.*

(iv) *Examination of case studies*: a number of case studies of development control decisions were identified from the literature, from interviews with local authorities, and by a search of planning appeal decisions in the last two years. These case studies were selected as examples where pollution and waste management featured in the planning decision. They were reviewed to identify how pollution and waste issues were treated in the planning process. In total over forty cases were examined and those which best illustrate the issues are discussed in the *Appendix* to *Annex C. (Section C.6)*

(v) *Interviews with other bodies*: interviews were held with the principal pollution control agencies - HMIP and NRA - and with relevant departments of central government. Local Authority air pollution control and waste regulation officers were involved in many of the interviews conducted under (ii). A number of other organisations were also contacted who were expected to have information or views relevant to the research. A list of all the organisations contacted is given in *Annex D*, together with the names of the individuals who were interviewed. The results of the interviews are incorporated, as appropriate in *Annexes B* and *C*.

We wish to thank all those who contributed to the research for their frank and informative contributions to the work. We must also thank the members of the Steering Group established by the Department, which included individuals and representatives of many organisations and agencies, for their advice and guidance during the course of the research.

1.4   ORGANISATION OF THE REPORT

The remainder of this report is organised as follows.

*   *Section 2* explains the background to the study.

*   *Section 3* presents conclusions in relation to the five questions posed in the brief.

*   *Section 4* presents recommendations for the content and structure of the proposed PPG.

*   *Annexes A to D* present the detailed findings on which *Sections 3* and *4* are based.

    *   *Annex A* describes the current pollution control regimes;

    *   *Annex B* reviews the treatment of pollution and waste in development plans and the extent of consultation with pollution control agencies in plan making;

    *   *Annex C* reviews the treatment of pollution and waste issues in development control including the role of consultations and EA;

    *   *Annex D* is a Bibliography, together with a list of Local Authorities, regulatory agencies and other bodies interviewed, and a list of the development plans reviewed.

> *"Planning control is primarily concerned with the type and location of new development and changes of use. Once broad land uses have been sanctioned by the planning process, it is the job of pollution control to limit the adverse effects that operations may have on the environment. But in practice there is common ground. In considering whether to grant planning permission for a particular development, a local authority must consider all the effects, including potential pollution; permission should not be granted if that might expose people to danger."*
>
> This Common Inheritance;   HMSO 1990

2.1   INTRODUCTION

Britain's Environment Strategy '*This Common Inheritance*' (1990) states that the Government takes a precautionary approach to the control of pollution relating the scale of effort to the degree of risks. It informs this approach with the best available scientific understanding and with sound economics. Its policy is to make available to the public full information about environmental issues and to involve the public in decision making. The Government will apply policies to:

- prevent pollution at source;
- minimise the risk of harm to human health and the environment;
- encourage and apply the most advanced technical solutions;
- apply a 'critical loads' approach to pollution, in order to protect the most vulnerable environments; and
- ensure that the polluter pays for the necessary controls.

The land use planning system is a framework of guidance, incentives and control designed to ensure that patterns of land use reflect the interests of the community as a whole. Policies for land use must weigh and reconcile priorities concerned with both development and conservation.

Development proposals are considered against criteria adopted by local planning authorities, including the statutory development plan, and in the light of other material considerations. In this context central Government's national and regional guidance form important material considerations.

2.2   THE PRESENT RELATIONSHIP BETWEEN PLANNING AND POLLUTION

The brief for this study notes that there is growing concern about the relationships between development and pollution and between the planning system and pollution controls. A number of factors have contributed to this concern.

- At the forefront must be the growing public awareness of pollution. It has traditionally been to the local authority that the public has turned in its efforts to prevent and control polluting development, and to the planning system as the most obvious mechanism for control. The elected local authority has the advantages of ready accessibility and responsiveness to democratic pressures, which it is perceived the pollution control authorities do not have.

- This perception is reinforced by the history of some aspects of pollution control in this country. Pollution control authorities outside the local government system have traditionally been perceived as 'too close to industry' and as unwilling to impose sufficiently strict controls, especially where industry might find difficulty in complying with those controls. As a result local authorities have not been confident in relying on the pollution control authorities to protect their interests, and have sought to exercise the necessary controls through the planning system.

- Local authorities have also been concerned that the powers of pollution control authorities are too narrow to protect the wider interests of the community. Matters which it is felt have been inadequately addressed through the pollution control regime include, for example, the effects of cumulative pollution from incremental development, the risks of pollution from unintended releases, the impact of perceptions of risk on the local community and on investor confidence, and the risks of non-compliance with pollution control measures.

- Public concerns about pollution and lack of confidence in the pollution control regime, have led to considerable pressure on planning officers to identify pollution risks as reasons for refusing planning permission or for imposing onerous conditions. Often these considerations were, without question, relevant to planning, but there have been occasions when it is argued that they go beyond the tests of relevance set out in Circular 1/85 [1] [2]. In these circumstances, uncertainty, recourse to appeal, and often lengthy public inquiries, have imposed considerable costs on the developer, on the public and on the planning system.

- Finally the introduction of Environmental Assessment has provided planning authorities with much more information on the pollution implications of certain types of development, providing for them more explicit opportunities to consider these issues in the development control process.

All of these factors have contributed to the increasing readiness of local authorities to incorporate policies to prevent pollution in development plans, to use pollution reasons as grounds for refusing planning consent, and to seek to control pollution from development through conditions and planning agreements.

---

[1]   See the Annex to Circular 1/85, paragraphs 16 to 19.

[2]   Documents are referred to in the body of the report by their conventional short titles. Full references are given in the Bibliography in *Annex D*.

This report makes frequent reference to the pollution control regimes. These regimes have recently undergone major change and we therefore provide a brief overview of the current position and how this compares with the previous regimes from which much of the practical experience to which we refer is drawn. It has not been our purpose to investigate these regimes in any detail and the information presented here must not therefore be considered as a definitive statement of the legal position.

2.3.1   *Consent Procedures*

There are three principal acts governing the control of pollution (ie. intentional releases to the environment) in this country:

- the Environmental Protection Act 1990 (EPA 1990), Parts I and II;

- the Water Resources Act 1991 (WRA 1991), Part III;

- the Control of Pollution Act 1974 (COPA 1974), Part I.

COPA 1974 Part I contains provisions which govern the licensing of waste disposal operations which will in due course be replaced by provisions in EPA 1990 Part II [1].

A brief overview of the consent procedures operated under each of these Acts is given in *Annex A*. Five regimes are described.

In brief summary they are as follows:

- *Integrated Pollution Control (IPC)*: Under EPA 1990 Part I, authorisation to operate certain polluting processes is required from HMIP. To obtain authorisation the operator must use the Best Available Techniques Not Entailing Excessive Cost (BATNEEC) to prevent or minimise the release of potentially harmful substances to air, water or land and to render any releases that do occur harmless. Where a process is likely to involve releases to more than one medium the Best Practicable Environmental Option must be adopted to minimise damage to the environment as a whole. Statutory environmental quality objectives must not be breached.

- *Local Authority Air Pollution Control*: Under EPA 1990 Part I authorisation to operate certain other polluting processes must be obtained from the local authority. This system relates only to releases to air but again the operator must use BATNEEC to prevent or minimise releases or to render them harmless, and statutory air quality objectives must be met.

- *Discharge Consent*: Under WRA 1991 it is an offence to discharge poisonous, noxious or polluting matter into water without the consent of

[1] Present proposals are for introduction of waste management licences under EPA 1990 in April 1993.

NRA (unless the discharge is governed by an IPC authorisation or a waste licence (see below)).

- *Site Licensing*: Under COPA 1974 a licence from the local Waste Regulation Authority is required to operate a waste disposal site (including waste handling and treatment). The WRA must be satisfied that the operation poses no danger to public health or safety and does not cause water pollution or serious detriment to local amenity. A waste disposal site must have a valid planning permission before a site licence can be granted.

- *Waste Management Licensing*: Under EPA 1990 Part II, a new regime will be introduced in due course to replace site licensing. This regime will apply also to keeping of waste. Under the new regime the WRA must be satisfied that the applicant is a fit and proper person and that the operation will not cause pollution of the environment, harm to human health or serious detriment to local amenity. EPA Part II also introduces a "Duty of Care" regarding waste.

Figure 2.2*a* illustrates how these different regimes apply to development.

These regimes provide the basis for preventive control of pollution in this country. Between them they provide a system for prior consent to most intentional releases of polluting substances to air, water and land.

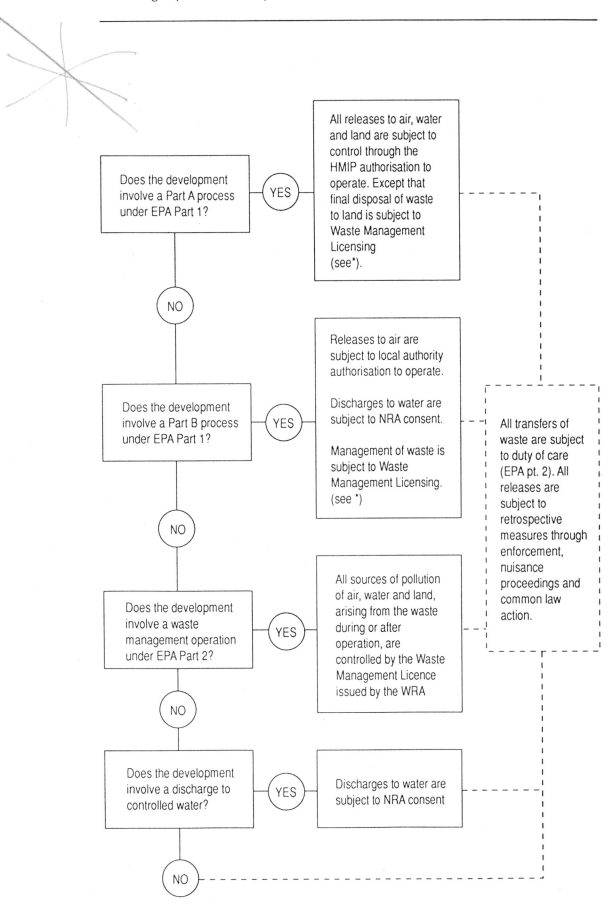

B

3.1   INTRODUCTION

This section presents our conclusions on the relationship between planning controls and pollution and waste management controls. The recommendations which flow from these are presented in *Section 4*.

The brief for the study identified five questions (see *Section 1.1*) to be addressed by the research:

Our conclusions are presented in relation to these five questions.

3.2   HOW HAVE POLLUTION AND WASTE BEEN TAKEN INTO ACCOUNT IN DEVELOPMENT CONTROL?

3.2.1   *How Do Pollution Issues Feature As Material Considerations In Planning Decisions?*

The evidence from our research indicates that planning authorities frequently consider pollution as an issue in the determination of planning applications, and that this practice is becoming more widespread. The reasons for this include the growing public awareness of pollution as an issue, the perceived need to use the planning system to achieve certain pollution control objectives which seem not to be achievable through other regimes, and the explicit introduction of information about pollution issues into planning through the EA process.

Examples of pollution issues identified as grounds for refusal of planning permission include the following:

- Unacceptable risk to neighbouring residential and agricultural land and to underground water resources, arising from storage, use or release of polluting substances.

- The cumulative impact of new potentially polluting development alongside existing polluting development in the area.

- Prejudice to future use of neighbouring land resulting from the polluting potential of the proposal.

- Local worries about the risk to health and safety from an apparently polluting installation.

- The potential for complaints from residents about pollution.

- The practical feasibility of any operator complying with the complexity and detail of conditions that would be needed to achieve an adequate level of environmental protection.

- The previous record of the operator in breaching consent conditions under planning and site licensing.

- The fact that proposed pollution control technologies were not technically proven.

- The likelihood that the pollution control agencies would not adequately meet their obligations under environmental protection legislation.

In some instances there was no appeal against these reasons for refusal or imposition of conditions and the justification was not tested; other cases have gone to appeal but have yet to be determined.

Reasons for refusal which have been accepted by inspectors as proper material planning considerations include: the potential for complaints; the complexity of conditions needed to protect the environment and the feasibility of any operator complying with them; the unacceptability of risk to the environment; and the fears and anxieties of local residents.

In some cases the level of risk to the environment and the concerns of local people were considered to be sufficient grounds for refusal by Inspectors; in others they required that strict conditions were imposed to deal with the concerns (see *Section 3.4*).

In one case where the quality of enforcement by a pollution control authority was identified as grounds for refusal, this was rejected by the Inspector as not being a material consideration.

3.2.2   *Need and Alternatives*

The questions of need and alternatives were raised in a number of development control cases where pollution was an issue. In these cases the Inspectors typically indicated that need was a material consideration where it weighed in the balance against objections on pollution grounds.

In such cases the need must be one determined by a wider community requirement than simply the commercial interests of the developer. In cases where pollution concerns had to be weighed against a wider need, it was also proper for the availability of alternatives with lesser consequences for the environment to be considered in reaching a decision.

3.2.3   *Existing Guidance On Material Considerations*

Evidence presented by planning cases suggests that while there may be an underlying consistency in the way in which pollution issues are addressed, there is scope for variation produced by local circumstances. Reference to existing guidance on material planning considerations appears to acknowledge this. It advises that *'any consideration which relates to the development and use of land is **capable of being** a planning consideration'* (PPG 1) (our emphasis).

It also advises that although planning should not duplicate controls imposed through other regimes it may be quite proper for planning to intervene to control pollution:

- where the considerations material to the planning and pollution control regimes are substantially different and it would be unwise to rely on the alternative regime to protect planning interests (Circular 1/85);

- where the development presents such clear risks to the public that restrictions should be attached or permission refused (MPG 1); and

- where the general interest in the case is wider than the interests of those directly involved in the pollution control regime (Circular 2/85).

Circular 2/85 also advises that it is right for planning authorities to be alert to the possibility of pollution even though there is a separate regime for its control.

Furthermore, it is interesting to note that, in discussing the interface between planning and site licensing, Waste Management Paper 26 states that it is *'clearly desirable to establish before planning permission is granted that, with the necessary conditions, a landfill development is **likely to qualify** for licensing'* (our emphasis).

Finally the recent draft for a new PPG1 on General Policy and Principles deals with the issue of need:

> *'Generally, it is not the function of the planning system to interfere with or inhibit competition between users and 'investors in land, or to regulate the overall provision ... for particular uses for other than land-use planning reasons ... . If, however, the applicant can demonstrate that there is a **weighty global national or local need** for a particular type of development **in a specific location** that consideration may be sufficient to outweigh important planning objections which would otherwise be a sufficient basis for the refusal of planning permission'. (Our emphasis).*

3.2.4   Conclusions on Current Practice

It is clear from our research that matters to do with pollution are, and have been accepted as being, legitimate planning concerns. What is also clear, however, is that in practice, every case has to be evaluated on its individual merits. There is, quite properly, no clear boundary between planning and pollution control and the relevance of pollution considerations to each case will depend on the circumstances. What planning authorities do is to judge, for each individual application, what factors contribute to the case for and against development, and what weight needs to be given to them in reaching a decision. It is a feature of our planning system that the weight that may be assigned to different factors, varies between cases. It also varies between local and national levels. One function of the call-in and appeals procedures is to allow a different judgement to be applied, in cases where national interests may outweigh local interests.

3.3   HOW HAS ENVIRONMENTAL ASSESSMENT AFFECTED THE INTERFACE?

The significance of the Environmental Assessment (EA) process in planning is that it explicitly requires the local planning authority to take into account *inter alia* the likely polluting effects of the proposed project. The information to be provided by the developer is required, by EC Directive (EEC/85/337), to include "*likely significant effects....resulting from.... the emission of pollutants, the creation of nuisances and the elimination of wastes*".

The evidence of the impact of EA on planning decisions from our research was that many of the authorities consulted have received few Environmental Statements (ES), and then often not for what might be termed 'polluting development' in the terms of this research. For those cases where an ES was submitted for polluting development, a number of problems were highlighted:

- the inadequacy of the ES submitted particularly with regard to local detail;

- that the ES only argued in support of the application, as opposed to providing a balanced consideration of the issues;

- where the ES was a detailed document, the inability of the planning officers to deal with the technical information provided.

In the latter instances the planning authorities sought advice from the pollution control authorities, but experience suggested that this often did not meet their needs (see *Section 3.5*). As a result in most complex cases, the local authority commissioned consultants to advise on the impact of the development and relied on their advice to inform the decision. In such cases pollution considerations were usually cited as material to the planning decision.

The issue of outline planning applications and EA was raised by a number of interviewees. There was concern that outline planning applications could not provide sufficient information to allow the planning authority to reach a proper decision on the acceptability of a site, in principle, for a potentially polluting development. It was therefore suggested that outline applications for this type of development should not normally be accepted. Some authorities already adopt this principle internally, particularly for waste developments.

A broader question, encompassing EA, was frequently raised. This concerned the level of detail of environmental information needed at the planning stage, as compared to the pollution control consent stage. A number of interviewees suggested that some guidance on this aspect would be helpful. This could, for example, indicate to developers that the ES should provide the best information available at the time. Where design is not sufficiently advanced to allow firm predictions of releases and their impacts at the planning stage, it could advise that a 'worst case' estimate should be made for the purposes of the ES. It could also make clear to developers that the two procedures require rather different concerns to be addressed.

- An EA at the planning stage should be concerned with demonstrating that the proposal will not have **an unacceptable impact on the environment**.

- At the pollution control stage, HMIP in particular, will be concerned with evidence that the proposal is designed to release **the minimum possible amount of pollution** to the environment [1]. There is, therefore, the potential for IPC to apply much stricter standards, and there appears to be every expectation in HMIP that this will often be the case.

3.4   *HOW HAVE PLANNERS USED CONDITIONS AND AGREEMENTS TO CONTROL POLLUTION?*

The cases we have examined reveal three main circumstances where conditions or agreements are used to control pollution.

3.4.1   *Use Of Planning Instead Of Pollution Control*

The first is where it is accepted that planning is the only, or at least the simplest, means of achieving pollution control objectives. Two particular instances occur frequently.

- For waste disposal sites, the site licensing regime does not permit conditions to be imposed regarding post-closure pollution control and monitoring. Thus it has become normal practice for such requirements to be imposed through planning conditions and agreements. Many authorities have worked out, together with the local Waste Regulation Authority, standard conditions or agreements for this purpose and it is common for county planning and Waste Regulation Authorities to work closely together on planning and site licensing.

- For developments with a potential for impact on the aquatic environment, NRA frequently seeks to use the planning system to impose controls which cannot be readily achieved under its own powers. Most usually this applies to matters such as flood prevention, land drainage and nature conservation, where there is no other authorisation regime open to NRA. But, NRA also requests that conditions be imposed on planning consents relating to pollution prevention, where it may have its own powers to control these sources but they are less convenient.

---

[1]   For new processes - the minimum technically possible; for existing processes - the minimum not entailing excessive costs.

Recently NRA has specifically identifed one area where it is recognised that the pollution control regime cannot achieve the necessary controls, and that NRA must rely on the planning regime to achieve its objectives. In a recent draft on 'Policy and Practice for the Protection of Groundwater' it states that:

> 'Many developments may pose a direct or indirect threat to groundwater resources. Where planning permission is required (eg chemical stores, residential development, mineral extraction, industrial development) often the **only control** is by means of conditions on the permission documents, or by refusal of permission'. (Our emphasis).

3.4.2 Use of Planning as Well as Pollution Control

The second set of circumstances in which conditions are imposed is less straightforward. Examples include where conditions are proposed:

- to restrict the releases of pollutants from a site to keep the risk to neighbouring land or resources to an acceptable level;

- to restrict the activity which could be carried out on the site for similar reasons;

- to address specifically the fears and worries of local people;

- to impose a release limit which would run with the land, rather than be associated with a licence to operate which could be varied or expire;

- to impose a release limit, to meet the concerns of a planning authority that the pollution control authority would not adequately enforce their own controls.

Whilst there is an argument that planning is duplicating the controls imposed by the pollution control regime, the objectives of such controls are frequently claimed by planners to exist in a wider context than the strict pollution control remit of the regulatory agencies. As such they would claim these controls are complementary. A particular example would be where conditions were attached requiring monitoring and information, or requiring establishment of community liaison, to meet concerns about the risks presented by development.

Inspectors and the Secretary of State have supported planning authorities in adopting some of these types of conditions in a number of instances, suggesting that there are circumstances where this approach is legitimate. Existing guidance also indicates that such conditions can be acceptable.

- Circular 1/85 offers model conditions restricting noise at the boundary of a site which, by implication, could be applied to other emissions or releases.

- It also indicates that in very special circumstances it may be appropriate to impose a condition restricting changes in activity which would normally be permitted development. An example is given regarding the storage of

16

hazardous substances. However, it notes that such conditions should not be used where a more direct condition would achieve the purpose, for example by **restricting emissions from the site.**

- Circular 9/84 also provides that planning authorities may restrict the amount, type or location of hazardous substances on site because of the implications for adjoining land use, or to restrict what may happen in the future.

The two examples relating to conditions running with the land and to lack of surety about enforcement of pollution controls do, however, appear to go against existing guidance. Circular 1/85 states that *'A condition cannot be justified on the grounds that the local planning authority is not the body responsible for exercising a concurrent control, and therefore cannot ensure that it will be exercised properly. Nor ... that a concurrent control is not permanent but is subject to expiry and renewal.'*

3.4.3 *Conditions Relating to Matters of Detail*

The third circumstance is where conditions are used to require that details of pollution control measures not available at the planning stage be submitted to and approved by the planning authority, before the development can commence.

This approach is frequently recommended by NRA in response to consultation on planning applications. It will recommend to planning authorities that a planning condition be imposed for specified works to be carried out *'in accordance with details which shall be submitted to and approved in writing by the planning authority **in consultation with the National Rivers Authority** before the development commences'* (our emphasis) (NRA Thames Region). We did not come across any individual cases where such a condition had been imposed for water pollution control reasons although it is used for land drainage reasons.

The only identified case in which such a condition had been imposed on a pollution issue, related to a scheme for gas monitoring associated with development adjacent to a landfill site. At appeal the Inspector ruled that the condition was not acceptable as monitoring, in itself, could not provide a guarantee of safety. The **principle** of whether such conditions were acceptable was not therefore tested.

This approach is supported by Circular 1/85 which advises that a condition can be imposed requiring a specified action to be taken before development can proceed. This could relate to an aspect of the development not fully described in the planning application which must be submitted for approval, and implemented, before development can begin. It gives examples of the application of such conditions to drainage and noise control schemes. It is emphasised that such a condition can only be applied if there is a reasonable prospect of the action being taken.

3.4.4   *Conclusions*

It is evident from our review that planning authorities are adopting conditions which appear to duplicate powers available to the pollution control agencies. The main reasons for this appear to be lack of confidence that the agencies will impose strict conditions on the operation, and that the conditions might be relaxed if, for example, the plant expanded under permitted development rights. This lack of confidence will only change as HMIP, in particular, demonstrates the stringency of its controls.

It is nevertheless likely, that planning authorities will, in unusual circumstances, seek to use planning conditions to control releases.

We consider, however, that a more appropriate response in most cases, would be as follows: for the planning authority to impose a condition that planning permission could not commence until pollution control authorisations had been granted and that the developer should ensure that the planning authority was consulted at this stage and was given an opportunity to review the measures proposed. At that stage the planning authority would have an opportunity to review the impact of the proposal, and the implications of conditions attached to the pollution control consent for matters such as the layout or design of the site, operating methods and hours, traffic, chimney design, etc. This would have various benefits.

L.P.A. actively consulted — not just informed

- It would ensure that the local planning authority was actively consulted at the pollution control stage, instead of simply being informed, as a local authority, via the public register. (The requirement for consultation would be imposed on the developer as it could not be imposed upon the pollution control agencies as they would be third parties).

any changes introd. by poll.cont. which although not require P.P. could be considered.

- It would ensure that any changes to the proposals introduced for pollution control purposes, which might have planning implications but which would not require planning permission, could be considered by the planning authority who could then alert the pollution control authority about any planning concerns. (An example would be increases in lorry traffic resulting from a switch from release to air to generation of waste introduced for BPEO reasons).

local concerns

- It would ensure that the planning authority was given a chance to flag up particular local concerns (eg sensitive local receptors, other pollution sources) to the pollution control authority, so that they could be taken into account in considering the pollution control application.

developers; earlier consulted

- It might encourage developers to consult the pollution control agencies at an earlier stage by prompting them to think about the implications of pollution control authorisation at the planning stage.

A further circumstance in which pollution control conditions might be acceptable, would be where the planning and pollution control agencies both agreed that planning was the best place for the requirements to be imposed.

3.5.1   *Objectives Of Consultation*

It is clear that planning authorities often do not have the technical expertise to evaluate the acceptability of potentially polluting development. In such cases they rely on the pollution control agencies to advise, or if they cannot or will not help, on outside consultants and other bodies.

In order to reach a decision an authority may need advice from the pollution control agencies on:

- whether the processes involved in a development are likely to be capable of satisfying pollution control requirements;

- the level of risk to people and the environment;

- what an unacceptable level of risk might be;

- what types of release might occur and what conditions might be set to limit the risk to acceptable levels in the particular location where the development is proposed;

- what aspects of pollution control, which could affect land use interests, might need to be reserved for later approval.

3.5.2   *Responses*

The nature of the response planners receive to consultation with pollution control agencies varies widely. Several problems have been highlighted:

- Responses are often slow, and when they are received it is too late to incorporate them.

- Responses often indicate 'no objection' but do not explain the basis on which the agency reaches this conclusion.

- Equally, responses registering an objection or recommending conditions may not explain the reasons.

- Responses may suggest that conditions should be imposed to achieve particular objectives, but do not explain what measures should be specified to achieve those objectives.

- Responses may state that the agency has received insufficient information to make a judgement.

- Responses are often quite clearly 'standard replies'. Planning officers sometimes have difficulty persuading members to give sufficient weight to such responses because they suggest the consultee has not addressed the particular circumstances of the individual case.

Some of these problems could be overcome if planning authorities:

- asked more specific questions;

- ensured, together with the agencies, that the information needed to reach a judgement was provided by developers; and

- understood how far agencies are able to respond at the planning stage.

3.5.3 Conclusions on Current Practice

With some consultees, particularly those located within local government, there is a good understanding about needs and expectations on both sides. Thus consultations with Waste Regulation Authorities and Local Authority Air Pollution Control often work effectively, especially where they are located close to the planning department in structural or geographical terms.

Concern was, however, expressed by local authority interviewees, that the close and effective cooperation between planning and Waste Regulation Authorities would be lost if waste regulation functions were transferred to a new Environment Agency. This reflected the wider concern about the lack of local democratic accountability of the pollution control agencies (HMIP, NRA) compared to local planning authorities.

Consultations with NRA also work reasonably well. Planning authorities have dealt with NRA and its predecessors over a long period and in some areas good working relationships have been established. Alongside this it has always been in NRA's interest to use the planning system to achieve certain of its objectives and NRA regions tend to take a very pro-active stance on liaison with planning. NRA has been criticised, however, for being slow in its response and for relying too much on standard replies. Experience on this seems to vary widely from area to area. The personal relationships between the individuals involved would appear to be important.

HMIP is in a rather different situation from the other agencies. The history of its predecessors, its apparent remoteness from local government, its recent establishment, and the fact that it is still drawing up its own procedures and guidance and putting resources in place, appear at present to militate against good collaboration between planners and the Inspectorate. Often planning authorities seek help from other organisations (eg consultants) where they might in other circumstances feel more able to call on HMIP.

Only time will tell how this relationship will develop. As yet there is not much experience of consultation with HMIP. Consultation is only mandatory in EA cases and the responses to non-statutory requests for advice have been mixed. The most usual response is that HMIP will ensure that adequate controls are imposed at the stage of IPC authorisation. HMIP is faced with a particular difficulty in that, until guidance is available on BATNEEC and BPEO for all IPC processes, inspectors, quite reasonably, are being cautious about the advice they are prepared to offer. It must also be understood that in order to reach a full judgement on any particular case HMIP needs much more information than would normally be available at the planning stage. Any advice they offer is, therefore, subject to major caveats.

Currently, there is a risk that planners will continue to be nervous about relying on the Inspectorate to properly protect their interests. Nothing in the guidance about the IPC system supports this lack of confidence, but this message is not reaching the planning community.

3.6.1   *Reference to Pollution in Development Plans*

Our review of development plans suggests that the degree to which pollution and waste management issues are addressed varies widely. In addition, the way in which such policies are included varies as does their scope and specificity. It is apparent, however, that in general the use of such policies is increasing. One particular factor has reinforced this, namely the undertaking of environmental audits by local authorities. Where an audit identifies environmental problems within a local authority area, the development plan provides one obvious vehicle for setting out policies for action. Many authorities are carrying out or are about to carry out such audits so that this trend seems likely to continue.

A number of general comments regarding pollution policies can be made.

3.6.2   *Strategic and General Policies*

Whilst many of the plans have an overall 'quality of life' theme as a dominant aim of the plan, few include pollution policies as part of their overall strategic policies.

Plans at all levels include general policies relating to pollution. These can be characterised either as a presumption against any development likely to cause pollution, or a presumption against development causing 'unacceptable' levels of pollution. Plans do not tend to define what is meant by the terms 'pollution' or 'unacceptable levels of pollution', although in one instance environmental quality objectives were specified by reference to other sources.

The types of pollution addressed by these policies are changing. This has emerged in two ways:

- The list of possible pollutants is being extended from noise, dust and fumes, which were traditionally identified by local planning authorities, to include, for instance, leachate and migrating gas.

- Policies are tending to move away from the traditional terminology of noise, dust and fumes and to refer, for example, to all emissions to air.

3.6.3   *Locational Policies*

Locational policies form the other main type of pollution-related policy. These relate to both potentially polluting development and to sensitive developments in the vicinity of existing polluting activity.

The policies are of three main types:

[handwritten margin note: land to →]

- policies allocating land as suitable for potentially polluting development;

[handwritten margin note: certain areas not]

- policies defining certain sensitive areas (eg aquifer protection zones) where potentially polluting development (either in general or of specific types) should not be permitted;

[handwritten margin note: housing not dev]

- policies specifying that certain types of sensitive development (usually housing) should not be permitted in the vicinity of polluting or hazardous installations or in areas severely affected by pollution. These may be general or refer to specific installations.

3.6.4 Current Guidance On Consideration Of Pollution Issues In Plans

Guidance on treatment of pollution issues in development plans is provided in PPG12. This indicates that plans must include policies and proposals which aim to protect and enhance high quality environments and improve poor environments. They may include policies *'designed to control pollution and to limit and reduce nuisances such as noise, smells and dirt'*. PPG12 notes that particular attention must be paid to protection of groundwater resources.

It further indicates that plans should take account of the location of existing hazardous installations and the need for new or relocated hazardous developments. Structure Plans may indicate areas where such developments may be acceptable, and detailed plans should set out criteria for control of new hazardous development and for location of other developments in the vicinity of hazardous installations.

Finally, the PPG requires the environmental appraisal of plans during their preparation.

3.6.5 Consultation On Development Plan Preparation

PPG 12 reminds local planning authorities that they are statutorily obliged to consult certain bodies at pre-deposit stage in plan preparation; these include other local authorities and the NRA. The PPG suggests additionally that *inter alia* HMIP should be consulted where aspects of the plan affect its interests.

In practice these bodies do appear to be consulted quite widely, along with many other organisations with an interest in pollution control. NRA is considering formulating model policies to be used as the basis for advice to planning authorities, although some authorities find their responses too voluminous and not sufficiently specific to the local area. It appears that as yet HMIP has not had much input into plan preparation.

3.6.6   *Waste Disposal*

We have reviewed treatment of waste disposal as a specific issue in development plans. Many Structure Plans and UDPs include policies on waste, most in separate chapters and some together with pollution or environmental policies. Some examples of separate minerals and waste plans, and two examples of joint planning/COPA Waste Disposal Plans were identified.

Where there was a COPA Waste Disposal Plan available at the time of preparation of the Structure Plan or UDP, it seems that this was taken into account in formulating planning policies on waste, although the WDP was not specifically referred to in most cases.

Policies on waste disposal tend to adopt a criteria based rather than location specific approach, in order to avoid political difficulties and, in particular, problems associated with blight. Policies indicate the criteria to be considered, in determining applications for waste operations and these include need, air quality, noise levels, water resources and gas generation alongside other planning issues. Interestingly one authority includes the past record of the operator as a factor to be considered in evaluating waste disposal proposals. Most authorities include policies on use of conditions and agreements to control waste disposal activities, through planning and/or site licensing. These policies recognise the close collaboration between planning and waste regulation which takes place in many authorities.

Some Structure Plans have also introduced policies on waste which promote recycling and waste minimisation, for example, indicating that the County Council will monitor waste generation in the area, follow new developments in recycling technology, and support recycling initiatives. Only one authority was identified that included a policy that waste disposal arrangements should be considered when a major project is proposed.

Some authorities are in the course of preparing Waste Local Plans under the Planning and Compensation Act. One county that had prepared a joint planning/COPA Waste Disposal Plan in the early 1980's understood that it would now be required to prepare separate plans.

English District Local Plans do not typically include policies on waste as they are not the planning authority. Policies indicating how districts will respond when consulted on proposals affecting their area were identified although PPG 12 indicates that this is not a local matter.

3.6.7   *Guidance on Planning and Waste*

Many of the authorities interviewed identified matters relating to planning and waste where they would welcome guidance. These included:

- definition of waste;

- definition of waste disposal operations re county matters and re use classes (eg scrapyards, recycling plants, wastewater treatment plants);

- the scope of waste local plans and their relationship to waste disposal plans, and whether a joint Waste Local and Waste Disposal Plan would be acceptable;

- criteria for location of waste management and disposal operations;

- planning of after use of waste disposal sites (is it a county or district matter?);

- use of conditions on post-closure pollution control after introduction of the new waste licensing regime;

- policies on self-sufficiency and import/export of waste;

- waste minimisation and waste generation as issues in development control;

- planning of development in the vicinity of landfill sites.

In spite of the existence of statutory provisions and guidance on these issues, this is evidently an area where planning officers and authorities have some difficulty.

C

4　　　*RECOMMENDATIONS*

On the basis of the research findings summarised in *Section 3* we have
identified a number of topics which we recommend should be addressed in
the proposed PPG. We also set out a proposed structure for the PPG.

4.1　　　*EXPLAINING THE OTHER REGIMES*

One frequent reason why planning authorities concern themselves with
pollution is a lack of confidence that the pollution control regimes will
protect planning interests. An essential task for the PPG should be to
explain these other regimes and the extent to which they can be expected to
protect land use planning interests. It should provide planners with a clear
understanding of the scope of the other regimes, the factors that must be
taken into account by the agencies in deciding whether or not to grant
authorisation, and the objectives that must be met before authorisations or
consents are granted. *Annex A* of this report provides a first attempt at
presenting this information.

4.2　　　*IMPROVING THE CONSULTATION PROCESS*

Improvements in consultation with pollution control agencies appear to be a
second key to solving problems at the interface with planning.

Better collaboration would have benefits for planning - upgrading the quality
of advice available to planners, improving the confidence planners feel in the
agencies - and possibly for pollution control, by facilitating early discussions
on the pollution control requirements of development.

The PPG could assist this process in several ways by:

- ensuring that planners and pollution control agencies are aware of the
  statutory requirements for consultation, and that planners are aware of
  other organisations who may be able to assist;

- encouraging planners to consult extensively and to use a wide range of
  resources to assist them when needed, including sources of assistance
  other than the agencies (such as local or national centres of expertise,
  interest groups, consultants);

- providing guidance to planners, and through them developers, on the
  advice agencies are able to provide, and on the questions they should ask
  to elicit the necessary response (see below);

- providing guidance to planners and through them developers, on the
  information the agencies are likely to need to answer their questions; in

particular, this should emphasise the need to provide information on local issues and concerns of which the agencies may be unaware; and

- advising developers about the value of early consultation with the pollution control agencies, in facilitating the planning process.

Particular questions which it would be useful for local planning authorities to ask of consultees in relation to pollution control might include:

- whether the development in the form in which it is proposed is likely to be capable of authorisation under pollution control legislation;

- what types of pollution are likely to be associated with the development (where this information is not already provided by the developer in an ES);

- whether pollution from the development is likely to significantly affect any particularly sensitive receptors in the vicinity; for this purpose the consultation request should identify any sensitive receptors near the proposed site - homes, hospitals, schools, natural habitats, recreation sites, etc;

- what the requirements of BATNEEC are likely to be for the development in question.

The PPG should reinforce the guidance given on early consultation in cases subject to EA and extend it to developments which, although potentially polluting, do not require EA. In some areas informal relationships and procedures facilitate the consultation process. The PPG should encourage planners to develop such arrangements where possible.

Although the PPG is formally addressed only to planning authorities, it will be important to consider its likely wider audience in drafting. Thus the PPG could usefully address itself to the consultees as well as the planners on consultations regarding pollution control. The pollution control agencies should be encouraged to start discussions with developers and planning authorities at an early stage, and to provide as much information and advice as possible on the basis of their best judgement, without compromising their later consideration of pollution control authorisations.

4.3   MATERIAL CONSIDERATIONS

We have noted in *Section 3* the need for clarification on the role of pollution control issues as material considerations in planning. We highlighted our conclusion that, although the PPG might indicate certain issues that should or should not be material considerations, it would be as useful to recognise explicitly that there is a "grey area" between planning and pollution. Within that area planning authorities must exercise their discretion, with appropriate support from the pollution control agencies.

In exercising that discretion we consider that there are four questions which planning authorities should seek to answer for potentially polluting development.

- whether the development, in the form in which it is proposed at the planning stage, is **capable of being designed and operated in a manner which is reasonably likely to be authorisable** under pollution control legislation;

- whether the development presents **such a level of risk to neighbouring land uses** (including people, water resources on or under the ground, commercial operations and natural systems) - either through the nature of the source of risk or the sensitivity of the receptor - that it is an inappropriate use of the land in question;

- whether the development is **perceived to present such a risk to neighbouring land uses and that risk cannot properly be allayed by reference to objective or accepted standards**, that it would harm the current use of the land or prejudice the planning authority's aspirations for its future use as set out in the development plan;

- whether, if there are important planning objections on pollution grounds, there is a **weighty global, national or local need** sufficient to outweigh those objections, and if there is such a need, whether there is a **reasonable alternative** to the proposal which would cause lesser pollution impacts.

In determining the answers to these three questions planners should seek the advice of the pollution control agencies and other bodies.

We have noted in *Section 4.1* our recommendation that the PPG should provide a description of the pollution control regimes for planners. Although planners are the primary audience for PPGs, we suggest that the opportunity should also be taken to explain the remit of the planning regime to the other agencies and to developers. From our own experience we are aware that many developers are confused by the apparent overlap between the different regimes. It will be important to convey the basic objective of planning, that is to ensure the appropriate use of land, and to explain that any matter which could affect the use of land, including pollution, is capable of being a material planning consideration.

4.4   PLANNING CONDITIONS

We recommend that the PPG should give the following guidance on planning conditions regarding pollution:

- That planning conditions should not be used where they would duplicate pollution control measures, except in exceptional circumstances where there is a clear and demonstrable need to protect planning interests not adequately protected by the pollution control regime [1].

- That a planning condition to achieve pollution control may be used where it is agreed by the pollution control and planning agencies that the planning permission is the appropriate place for the requirement to be imposed.

- That where a planning authority is concerned, for legitimate planning reasons, about the requirements that will be imposed under the pollution control regime, or about the effect of those requirements on layout, design or activity at the site, then it may impose a condition that planning permission shall not commence until the development has received approval under specified pollution control legislation, and that the developer must ensure that the planning authority is consulted at that stage and given an opportunity to review the measures proposed and make representations to the pollution control agency if appropriate.

This last provision, allowing for consultation of the local planning authority at the time of pollution control consents, would go some way towards responding to local authorities concern about the lack of local accountability within the pollution control regime operated by HMIP.

We recommend that the existing guidance in Circular 1/85 should still apply; that is that conditions cannot be justified on the grounds either that the planning authority cannot ensure that other controls will be properly exercised, or that the other controls may be varied over time.

Finally it should be noted that it is existing policy that a local planning authority should refuse planning permission in cases of doubt, rather than rely on conditions to control risk.

4.5   *CONSULTATION ZONES AROUND POLLUTING DEVELOPMENT*

It has been suggested to us that a consultation approach similar to that used for major hazard installations could be adopted for IPC installations. This would involve HMIP and the local planning authority establishing a **Consultation Zone** around each installation. Any proposals for new development within that zone would then be subject to consultation with HMIP on the potential risk before grant of planning permission. We consider that this proposal has merit but, if it is to operate in the same way as the system operated by HSE for major hazards, it will involve HMIP in

---

[1]   One example, would be where there was an indirect threat to groundwater from storage or use of substances on a site, but there was no direct discharge. There would be no requirement for discharge consent from NRA because there was no prior intent to discharge. Therefore unless the site was subject to IPC, there would be no pollution control authorisation attached to it. This circumstance has been recognised by NRA and the Authority intends to use the planning system to exercise control.

A second example, might be where the use of a hazardous material on site is adequately regulated by the pollution control agencies, but there remain land use planning concerns about the pollution risks associated with the transport of that material to the site, perhaps through neighbouring residential areas.

considerable additional work. Like HSE, HMIP will have to establish the basis for defining Consultation Zones, define them for each installation, prepare internal guidance on how to assess the risk to applications within those zones, and then provide advice to planning authorities on each application. Setting up this system will therefore be a considerable task.

4.6 OTHER ISSUES ON DEVELOPMENT CONTROL

There are three specific pieces of advice which could be considered for inclusion in the PPG:

- That planning authorities should be advised not to accept **outline applications** for specified types of polluting development. These could be defined as developments which will subsequently require IPC authorisation and those requiring EA. This recommendation would follow what is happening in practice in many authorities.

- That planning authorities should be advised to request information from developers, at the time of the planning application, on any **pollution control authorisations** which would subsequently be required. This would alert planners to the need for consultation.

- That planning authorities should be encouraged to respond when, as local authorities, they are informed through the **public register** of applications under EPA 1990 and WRA 1991, which raise issues relevant to planning and use of land. This route could be used to inform HMIP and NRA of particular local concerns which they should take into account when determining applications for pollution control authorisations.

4.7 DEVELOPMENT PLANNING

It is clear that planning authorities are actively taking pollution issues into account in Development Plans. This is supported by PPG12. Consideration should be given to expanding upon the guidance in PPG12 in a number of areas.

- **Policies on the location of potentially polluting development.** This should cover policies directing certain types of expected development to suitable areas, and away from sensitive areas, and policies establishing criteria for location of different types of polluting development.

- **Consultation in development plan preparation.** This should reinforce the guidance in PPG 12 about statutory and informal consultation with pollution control agencies and could expand upon this by informing both planners and pollution control agencies on what is needed and what can be expected from each side. (See *Section 4.2*).

We consider it particularly important that planning authorities should be advised to make provision for types of polluting development which are expected in their areas. This will follow the principle established for wastewater treatment plants in guidance issued in 1991. It should ask planning authorities to consider the implications of national and regional guidance for such development in their areas.

4.8   REGIONAL PLANNING GUIDANCE

Regional Planning Guidance (RPG) is taking on increasing importance in the planning system. RPGs provide a vehicle for establishing targets for provision of land for specified purposes and the allocation of those targets between county and metropolitan areas. RPG's currently set targets mainly for housing provision.

However where it is possible to identify needs for potentially polluting development on a regional basis, they could also be used to direct that development to the most appropriate areas, or to establish regionally derived criteria for siting. One area in which this could be appropriate and feasible, would be in identifying provisions for waste management facilities, in accordance with requirements for regional self-sufficiency.

4.9   PLANNING AND WASTE

We have indicated that, during our research, a number of areas relating to planning and waste have been identified, on which local authorities would welcome guidance. Many of these do not relate to the polluting aspects of waste and have not therefore been investigated in any detail. Nevertheless the need for guidance still exists. The matters referred to are identified in 3.6.6.

4.10   GENERAL ISSUES AND STRUCTURE OF THE PPG

We have three general recommendations on the proposed PPG.

- The PPG should be short. Several interviewees indicated that they were having difficulty in dealing with the volume of guidance directed to them.

- The PPG should be addressed to the pollution control authorities and to developers as well as to the planning authorities, either formally or informally, so that they are aware of their part in the process.

- There is an evident need for particular guidance on planning waste disposal operations. We recommend therefore that consideration be given to preparing a separate PPG, or to separating the planned PPG into two sections:

  - Planning and Pollution: this would deal with the interface between the planning and pollution control regimes for all types of development, including waste disposal operations.

- Planning and Waste Disposal: this would deal with the full range of issues confronted in planning waste disposal operations. This would include their pollution potential, where there are some special issues affecting waste disposal such as landfill gas and leachate control, but also other environmental protection issues such as nature conservation, landscape protection, noise, transport, bird nuisance, litter, etc, and other issues such as the relationship between planning and site licensing, definitions of waste and waste disposal, the relationship between waste local plans and waste disposal plans, planning of after-use of waste sites, and so on.

Further proposals for the structure of the PPG are set out in *Table 4.9a*.

Finally, our research has suggested that there is considerable guidance available in existing circulars, PPG's and other government documents. Much of this is sound and there is a case for consolidating relevant elements of it in one place.

Table 4.9a   *Proposal for Structure of the PPG*

Part I Planning and Pollution Control

Preface:	Policy principles on pollution control (reference to White Paper, precautionary principle etc).
1. **Defining the Problem**:	Why are planning authorities concerned about pollution
2. **Explaining the Interface**:	What are the relative responsibilities of the different agencies? Planning - pollution control
3. **Pollution and Development Planning:**	Pollution policies - area policies, siting criteria, providing for polluting development, relationships to waste planning, consultations, role of regional guidance
4. **Pollution and Development Control:**	Pollution issues in development control, key questions, material considerations, conditions and agreements, consultations.
5. **Pollution and EA:**	Treatment of pollution in EA
6. **Other Guidance:**	Outline applications, seeking information on authorizations,pollution registers

Part II Planning and Waste

Preface: policy principles on waste management.

1. **Waste and waste disposal in the planning regime.**

2. **The planning, waste regulation and pollution control regimes.**

3. **Waste local plans.**

4. **Development control and waste.**

Annex A

The Pollution Control Regimes

POLLUTION CONTROL AGENCY: Her Majesty's Inspectorate of Pollution (HMIP).

ACTIVITIES SUBJECT TO CONTROL: A list of prescribed processes is defined in the Environmental Protection (Prescribed Processes and Substances) Regulations 1991 SI 1991/472. These processes are prescribed because, typically, they involve the potential release of polluting substances to air and/or water and/or land. From April 1991 all **new or substantially altered** processes are subject to IPC. A programme has been established for bringing existing processes under the IPC regime.

FORM OF CONSENT: An operator of a prescribed process must hold an authorisation to operate that process from HMIP, unless it can be demonstrated that the process releases only trivial amounts of polluting substances. The authorisation may be subject to conditions. It can be revoked or altered at any time by HMIP and is granted for a limited period (at most four years). The operator must notify HMIP if the authorisation is transferred to another party.

MATTERS TO BE CONSIDERED IN GRANTING CONSENT: HMIP must be satisfied that the operator:

- is using best available techniques not entailing excessive costs (BATNEEC) to prevent releases of prescribed substances to air, water and land, to minimise those releases if they cannot be prevented, and to render harmless releases of any substances that do occur;

- is using the best practicable environmental option (BPEO) to minimise the harm caused by these releases (eg ensuring that substances are released to the medium(s) where they will cause least harm);

- is capable of complying with the conditions imposed upon the authorisation;

and that the release of any substances which is permitted will not cause any statutory environmental quality objectives (EQO's) to be exceeded. HMIP must take NRA's advice on achievement of water quality objectives.

"Harm" is defined as:

- harm to the health of living organisms or other interference with the ecological systems of which they form part;

- offence to any of man's senses or harm to his property.

"Harmless" has the corresponding meaning.

For new processes the BATNEEC requirement translates effectively into a requirement to use BAT, with the proviso that the additional cost of moving to a stricter form of control must not be out of proportion to the environmental damage avoided.

In making a decision on an individual application, HMIP must consider the guidance issued for the process (which will indicate BAT options, emission limits and BPEO considerations), any relevant EQO's, the individual characteristics of the process, the assessment of options and their environmental impact provided by the operator, and the particular local conditions, including the potential for cumulative impact with existing sources in the area. HMIP guidance indicates that BATNEEC for **preventing and minimising releases** should be equivalent for similar processes irrespective of location, but that BATNEEC **for rendering any releases harmless** may take account of local circumstances.

Cont'd

Guidance notes will eventually be issued for all prescribed processes. But in the interim, regional inspectors are advised to seek advice from HMIP headquarters on processes for which there is no guidance, in order to ensure consistency of approach.

CONDITIONS: Authorisation will be granted subject to conditions on the use of particular techniques or on compliance with particular emission limits.

NB Under EPA 1990 "techniques" is interpreted widely, to include process design, design, layout and maintenance of the facility, operating procedures and practices, quality assurance measures, numbers, qualifications and training of personnel, supervision of personnel, monitoring and record keeping.

CONSULTATIONS: Applications for authorisation under IPC must be advertised locally, placed on the public register at HMIP regional office, sent to the local district council for placing on the local public register, and sent to statutory consultees. Local authorities are not statutory consultees. Any representations made by any individual or organisation, must be taken into account by HMIP. If an IPC process involves the final disposal to land of waste, HMIP must notify the Waste Regulation Authority (See *Box A3*).

POLLUTION CONTROL AGENCY: Local Authority (functions usually carried out by Environmental Health Department or equivalent).

ACTIVITIES SUBJECT TO CONTROL: A list of prescribed processes subject to local authority control is defined in the Environmental Protection (Prescribed Processes and Substances) Regulations 1991 SI 1991/472. These processes are prescribed because typically they involve the potential for release of polluting substances to air. A programme has been established for bringing existing processes under the regime by 1992. All new processes are subject to local authority control from April 1991.

FORM OF CONSENT: An operator of a Part B prescribed process must hold an authorisation to operate that process from the local authority, unless it can be demonstrated that the process generates trival amounts of polluting substances released to air. The authorisation may be subject to conditions. It can be revoked or varied at any time and must be reviewed at least every 4 years. The operator must notify the authority if the authorisation is transferred to another party.

MATTERS TO BE CONSIDERED: The local authority must be satisfied that the same requirements are met as for Part A IPC processes, except that as the authorisation is concerned only with releases to air, the BPEO obligation does not apply. The same factors must be taken into account by the local authority in making a decision on an individual application.

CONDITIONS: The same principles apply as under Part A.

CONSULTATIONS: The same principles apply as under Part A except that there are fewer statutory consultees under LAAPC than IPC.

POLLUTION CONTROL AGENCY: National Rivers Authority (NRA)

ACTIVITIES SUBJECT TO CONTROL: It is an offence to knowingly cause or permit any poisonous, noxious or polluting matter, or any solid waste, to enter any controlled waters, without the consent of the NRA (unless the discharge is governed by an IPC authorisation or a Waste Disposal or Waste Management Licence (See *Boxes A4 and A5*). Therefore any activity where it is the intention to make such a discharge is subject to this regime.

Controlled waters are defined in the Act to include most surface water bodies and groundwater. If a discharge is made to a public sewer, it will be subject to conditions imposed by the sewerage undertaker. It will then be for the sewerage undertaker to ensure that the resulting discharge to the receiving water meets the conditions of his consent.

FORM OF CONSENT: Anyone making such a discharge must hold a discharge consent from NRA. The consent may be subject to conditions. It may be revoked or varied at any time and must be reviewed from time to time (not more frequently than 2 years after grant of consent).

The consent and any conditions attached, apply to any person making the discharge, not just to the person to whom the consent was originally granted.

MATTERS TO BE CONSIDERED IN GRANTING CONSENT: In deciding whether or not to grant consent and if so, under what conditions NRA must be satisfied:

- that statutory water quality objectives will be met;
- that the discharge will not lead to a significant deterioration in water quality or adversely affect legitimate downstream uses;

and it must take account of NRA's general duty to maintain and improve the quality of water. (These requirements are not set out in the Act but have been defined based on discussion with NRA).

NRA takes into account the cumulative effect of new and existing discharges on water quality and of local conditions and uses of the receiving water.

There are no obligations under WRA 1991, regarding Best Available Techniques or Best Practicable Means. NRA is cognisant of the impact of its requirements on dischargers, but seeks to prevent difficulties arising by using prior informal discussions to change proposals or discourage applicants from applying in circumstances where this might be the case.

CONDITIONS: Consent may be given subject to conditions. These may concern:

- the location, design and construction of the outlet;
- the nature, origin, composition, volume, rate and timing of the discharges;
- the steps to be taken to minimise the polluting effect of the discharge, including treatment or any other process affecting the discharge. (This does not, however, extend upstream of so-called end-of-pipe treatment eg to conditions relating to the production process generating the discharge).
- sampling, keeping records and provision of information to NRA.

CONSULTATIONS: On receipt of an application NRA must *inter alia*, place the application on the public register, publish a notice of the application locally and in the London Gazette, and send a copy to the local authority, unless NRA considers that the discharge will have not appreciable effect on the receiving waters. Any representations or objections must be considered.

The provisions described below will apply until such time as SS 35-44 of EPA 1990 are implemented (see *Box A5*)

POLLUTION CONTROL AGENCY: The County Waste Regulation Authority (EPA 1990 Part II).

ACTIVITIES SUBJECT TO CONTROL: COPA 1974 Part I applies to deposit of household, commercial and industrial waste on any land and to use of plant or equipment to deal with waste (this includes most types of waste handling and treatment including transfer, recovery and incineration, but excludes storage except for certain special wastes - See however, Waste Management Licensing, *Box A5*)

FORM OF CONSENT: All operations involving treatment or disposal of waste require a licence issued by the WRA. The licence will specify conditions. A site licence may be varied or revoked at any time and Waste Management Paper 4 indicates that it should be fully reviewed every five years or sooner. A licencee wishing to transfer the licence to another party much advise the WRA in advance of the transfer.

MATTERS TO BE CONSIDERED IN GRANTING CONSENT: The WRA must be satisfied that the operation:

* poses no danger to public health and safety;
* does not cause water pollution;
* does not become seriously detrimental to the amenities of the locality;

and can impose conditions to achieve these aims. Conditions will reflect local circumstances and take account of best practicable practices at the site and as indicated by Waste Management Papers. A licence can, however, only be **refused** on grounds of danger to public health or water pollution, not on grounds of amenity.

Licensing is concerned with the day-to-day operation of the site. To ensure that broader considerations relevant to development are addressed it is a pre-requisite of licensing that the site has planning permission. This will set the framework within which the facility will operate but should not seek to impose operational conditions which are more appropriate to the licence.

Licence conditions apply to the licence holder and apply only for the duration of the licence (which can be handed in at any time). It is therefore usual for the planning system to be used to control aftercare of the site in order to achieve planning objectives for subsequent use of land. WMP 4 explains that there may be some difficulties in using conditions for monitoring and control of gas and leachate, particularly with regard to enforcement. Some authorities therefore ask applicants to include details in their applications, or use planning agreements.

CONDITIONS: The licence is granted under two parts:

* Part 1 sets out operational criteria;
* Part 2 sets out the practices to be adopted to meet these criteria, including a working plan.

Conditions may govern waste types and quantities, site preparation and infrastructure, notices and fences, site operation, monitoring and inspection.

CONSULTATIONS: The WRA must consult NRA and HSE, and other parties if it wishes, but there is no requirement to advertise the application or place it on a public register.

A5

The provisions described below have not yet been implemented. They will replace the COPA Site Licensing regime described in *Box A4*.

POLLUTION CONTROL AGENCY: The Waste Regulation Authority.

ACTIVITIES SUBJECT TO CONTROL: Waste Management Licencing will apply to deposit, treatment, keeping or disposing of household, commercial and industrial waste. (The principal change from COPA is the extension to **keeping** waste). It should be noted that a waste management operator may also require authorisation under EPA Part I (IPC or LAAPC) and vice versa, but a Part I IPC authorisation cannot regulate the final disposal in or on land of waste. So the functions of the Waste Management Licence cannot be duplicated by IPC.

FORM OF CONSENT: It will be an offence to deposit, treat, keep or dispose of waste (including knowingly causing or permitting), without a waste management licence. The licence will be granted to the occupier and may be subject to conditions. The licence may be varied or revoked at any time, although in revoking a licence the licence holder's obligations for aftercare may remain in force if required by the WRA. The guidance on full review at least every 5 years (WMP 4) is expected to continue to apply. A Waste Management Licence may be transferred to another party with the approval of the WRA, following a joint application by both parties.

MATTERS TO BE CONSIDERED IN GRANTING CONSENT: The WRA must satisfy itself:

- that an extant planning permission is in force for the land, or that there is an established use certificate;

- that the applicant is a fit and proper person;

- that the operation will not cause:

  - pollution of the environment;
  - harm to human health;
  - severe detriment to local amenity;

  except that a licence application cannot be refused on the grounds of the last consideration if there is a planning permission in force, (as opposed to an established use certificate) as it is considered that the planning system will have addressed local amenity issues.

"Pollution of the environment" means release into any environmental medium of substances resulting from the waste which are capable of causing harm to man or any other living organisms supported by the environment.

"Harm" is defined as under EPA Part I (see *Box A1*).

These requirements can be compared with those under COPA which relate to pollution of water rather than pollution of the environment, and to danger to public health and safety rather than harm to human health, man or any other living organisms.

Unlike COPA site licensing, Waste Management Licences are concerned with circumstances prior to and after the actual operations involving waste, including aftercare arrangements. In theory there may, therefore, be less need to use the planning system to impose aftercare requirements under the new regime. (In practice, it has been suggested that it may prove easier to ensure financial guarantees are provided through planning agreements and they may continue to be used).

The requirement that an operator must be a fit and proper person must be judged in relation to:

- previous operation of the activity;
- fulfilment of previous licence conditions;
- previous relevant convictions;
- technical competence;
- financial competence.

Financial competence requires a judgement of whether the applicant can finance the obligations imposed by the licence including any relating to aftercare.

CONDITIONS: Licence conditions may relate to activities authorised by the licence, to precautions which must be taken, and to works to be carried out **before, during or after**, the main operations.

CONSULTATIONS: Before granting a waste management licence the WRA must consult NRA and HSE and take any representations made into account. There is no requirement to inform the planning authority in England and Wales as it will be the same authority (in Scotland there is a requirement to consult the planning authority which will be the district council, implying therefore, that consultation with the planning authority is intended to occur).

Annex B

Development Planning

This Annex presents the results of the review of development plans which was undertaken to determine their approach to pollution and waste issues. Both the policies included in the plans and the rationale for their adoption were examined. The review also considered how far planning authorities have taken account of any relevant waste disposal plan in drawing up their development plan.

Reviewing the policies stated in the development plans, though important, does not necessarily give a full picture of the way in which these policies are implemented or used in practice. The Annex therefore draws also on the interviews with local planning authorities and other agencies to highlight key issues in the approach to pollution and waste policies in development plans.

The remainder of this Annex is organised as follows.

- *B2* presents the basis of the review of development plans;
- *B3* examines the current extent of planning guidance on this topic;
- *B4*, *B5* and *B6* successively present analyses of policies contained in Structure Plans, Unitary Development Plans and Local Plans;
- *B7* summarises the issues emerging from the review.

This review of development plans does not attempt a formal content analysis on the lines of earlier work commissioned by the Department of the Environment (Cross *et al* 1988), but a wider ranging examination of the plans to establish their coverage of and approach to pollution and waste. The analysis was done in two stages: an initial examination according to a broad set of questions, followed by a more comparative approach within the three groups of Structure Plans, Unitary Development Plans, and Local Plans.

B2.1   *The Development Plans Reviewed*

The 1988 Report "*BPEO through the planning system*" by *Cross et al* had examined development plans according to "*the prominence of pollution control as a topic in the document being examined, and the amount of policy material covering pollution which it contained*" (2.2.2). They had accordingly classified them into three categories. These categories were used in the selection of development plans for this research, in order to offer a range of approaches to pollution. It was assumed that those authorities which in the mid-late 1980s had substantial pollution policies would still give prominence to pollution matters.

A selection of approximately 30 development plans was identified, involving about equal numbers of Structure Plans, Unitary Development Plans, and Local Plans, of which one third were from our interviewee authorities. Further selection was made on the basis of achieving a spread across the Standard Regions of England and Wales, and a spread of plans in the various stages of preparation (draft, submission/deposit, at inquiry/examination, modifications or approval/adoption).

In the event, eleven Structure Plans, seven UDPs, and ten Local Plans (eight of which were District-wide Local Plans) were reviewed. Eight of the Structure Plans were approved (although in the case of Warwickshire, no final document was available from the printers; the 1990 Plan was therefore used). All the UDPs were consultation drafts; the District -wide Local Plans were also either consultation drafts or deposit plans. The titles of the plans reviewed are given in *Annex D*.

B2.2   *Waste Disposal Plans And Waste Local Plans*

The research was not intended to examine Waste Disposal Plans prepared under COPA, although one of the questions being addressed (see *Section 1.1 Objectives*) is the extent to which relevant waste disposal plans have been considered in drawing up development plans. As explained in *B3.3*, the Planning and Compensation Act has introduced a new requirement for waste local plans to be prepared by County Councils in England; in Wales policies on waste are to be incorporated in Districts' local plans, and in metropolitan areas, in UDPs. Some counties had prepared waste local plans under the old regime, but there was not a consistent set, and therefore waste local plans as such have not been reviewed.

This section sets out existing relevant Government guidance on consideration of pollution and related issues in the development planning system.

B3.1   *REGIONAL GUIDANCE*

The Government has recognised that certain issues need to be considered on a scale wider than a single county. Regional Planning Guidance (Strategic Planning Guidance in Wales) covers these issues. Waste treatment and disposal is identified as a topic which should normally be dealt with in such guidance (PPG12; paragraph 2.6).

- Regional guidance for **West Yorkshire** refers to the need to select landfill sites to minimise pollution, and for the Districts to coordinate polices having regard to the Waste Disposal Plan, and to consult with the Joint Waste Management Authority (RPG2; para 22).

- In **Greater Manchester** site selection for waste disposal should *'recognise the essential interrelationship between disposal, site licensing and planning control'* (RPG4; para 16).

- In the case of **Merseyside** it is suggested that UDPs should indicate where landfill would not be suitable, as well as locations where new opportunities might be examined (PPG11; para 22).

- The guidance for **Greater London** is more specific stating that UDPs should make provision for facilities such as incinerators, recycling plants and transfer stations (RPG; para 82).

- A set of guidelines for waste disposal in the South East Region, prepared by **SERPLAN**, were endorsed by the Secretary of State in December 1987.

Current RPG's do not make reference to pollution other than by waste.

B3.2   *DEVELOPMENT PLANS*

Development plans, prepared by local authorities under the Planning and Compensation Act 1991, provide an essential framework for decisions, and are intended to convey a clear understanding of the weight to be given to different aspects of the public interest. The new Act makes clear that development control decisions are required to accord with the development plan unless material considerations indicate otherwise.

Under the new Act the development plan for a non-metropolitan area comprises:
- the structure plan, providing a broad framework;
- the district local plan, containing detailed policies;
- the minerals local plan; and
- the waste local plan.

In metropolitan areas a unitary development plan covers both strategic and detailed policies and incorporates the waste local plan.

B3.2.1 *Structure Plans and UDP Part Is*

These provide a statement of how the county council will balance development and conservation objectives in different parts of its area. Policies are required for the improvement of the physical environment, and issues of waste disposal and the disposal of mineral waste are seen as key topics. Structure plans should also fully consider interactions between policies. For example, any relationship between waste disposal policies and policies for the conservation of the natural environment and amenity, would need to be taken account of in plan policies (PPG12; para 6.4 - 6.9). UDP Part I's should include similar policies in Metropolitan areas.

In drawing up development plans local authorities are to include land use and development policies designed to secure the conservation of natural beauty and the amenity of land. In addition:

- plans may include policies designed to control pollution and to limit and reduce nuisances such as noise, smells and dirt (para 6.18);

- particular attention should be paid to the protection of groundwater resources, the maps delineating areas of particular concern for groundwater, being drawn up by the NRA, should be taken into account in drawing up development plans (para 6.19);

- plans should take account of the effect of existing hazardous installations and the need for sites for new or relocated hazardous development. Proposals for sites to accommodate hazardous installations should be shown on proposals maps (para 6.20);

- plans should take into account the environmental effects of existing or proposed tipping operations (para 6.22).

Local Authorities are advised to consult with the following bodies at the pre-deposit stage:

- Her Majesty's Inspectorate of Pollution, on all proposals likely to involve environmental pollution;

- the National Rivers Authority, on matters relating to the availability of water resources, flood defences and land drainage, and on developments involving mining, the storing and deposit of waste, and the disposal of sewage or aqueous trade wastes;

- the Health and Safety Executive on all significant matters relating to health and safety including hazardous installations, licensed nuclear sites or licensed explosive factories.

B3.2.2   *Waste Local Plans*

The 1991 Act introduces a new requirement for local plan coverage for developments involving the depositing of refuse or waste materials. Counties, in England, are responsible for the preparation of a **waste local plan**, which they may combine with their minerals local plan. In Wales, districts are required to include waste policies in their district local plans. National Parks may choose between a separate waste local plan, or including the necessary policies in the Park-wide local plan, or minerals local plan. Waste local plans must be prepared for all areas by 1997.

B3.2.3   *Waste Local Plans and Waste Disposal Plans*

Waste local plans should set out authorities' detailed land use policies for the treatment of and disposal of waste, within the broad strategic framework of the structure plan. These plans are to state what regard they have had to the **waste disposal plan** which Waste Regulation Authorities have been required to draw up under COPA 1974 - a requirement strengthened by the Environmental Protection Act 1990. The two plans must therefore be complementary.

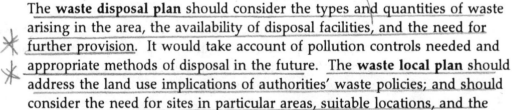

The **waste disposal plan** should consider the types and quantities of waste arising in the area, the availability of disposal facilities, and the need for further provision. It would take account of pollution controls needed and appropriate methods of disposal in the future. The **waste local plan** should address the land use implications of authorities' waste policies; and should consider the need for sites in particular areas, suitable locations, and the planning criteria likely to apply, including geological, hydrological and other considerations.

The guidance asserts that by taking into account the relevant waste disposal plans adequate provision can be made for waste disposal facilities such as landfill sites, incinerators or civic amenity sites, the need for which flows from the waste disposal plan. (PPG12; paras 3.13 - 3.15).

In a Consultation Paper '**Waste Disposal and Development Plans' (October 1990)**, the Department stated, '*The requirement to produce a development plan for waste disposal would not force authorities to identify each and every waste disposal site years in advance. Plans could stop short of individual site identification where this was sensible, but still serve a valuable planning function by setting out general criteria against which applications will be considered, indicating the main environmental and geological constraints, and identifying broad areas of search for sites and facilities*'.

The Consultation Paper also distinguished between **waste disposal plans**, which are subject to public consultation only, and **waste local plans** which are also subject to the public inquiry process. (In this context there is a concern that it is inappropriate to **require** that development plans should set down proposals fully consistent in nature, quality and distribution with those of waste disposal plans which have not been the subject of local public inquiry).

B3.2.4   *Other Development Plan Issues*

Circular 17/89 **'Landfill Sites - Development Control'** suggests that in preparing and reviewing development plans, authorities should take account not only of requirements for landfill sites, but also the implications of the presence of landfills for other development in the vicinity. County-district consultation, to assess the provision that can safely be made for other types of development in proximity to landfill sites (in the context of migrating gas), is urged. (Circular 17/89; para. 24).

Circular 21/87 **'Development of Contaminated Land'** states that contamination, or the potential for it, is a material planning consideration which is required to be taken into account in development plan preparation (Circular 21/87; para 5). It is noted that air and water pollution may occur from the disturbance of contaminants (Annex, para 1(c)). Development plans should set out policies for the reclamation and use of contaminated land. Local plans, and UDP Part IIs may include detailed criteria for determining planning applications, and may also set out site specific proposals so that they may be easily identifiable to landowners, and prospective purchasers or developers (Circular 21/87; Annex, para 9 and 10).

Circular 2/85 **'Planning Control over Oil and Gas Operations'** discusses the need to avoid duplication of planning and other controls. It goes on to say that the Government nevertheless 'accepts that pollution policies have a justifiable place in planning, and should be embodied in development plans where appropriate'. But planning conditions, it continues, should not be used to duplicate specific controls which already exist under pollution and other legislation (Circular 2/85; para. 17).

Circular 17/91 **'Water Industry Investment: Planning Considerations'** considers the land use implications of finding alternative means of disposal of sewage sludge currently deposited at sea. (The water companies are required to be using land-based disposal methods by the end of 1998). Local authorities are requested to consider in their development plans the need for sewage sludge storage areas and processing plant, and the role of incineration as an option, including associated requirements for the disposal of residual ash. The water companies are asked to consult local authorities well in advance over development programmes, so that they may be taken into account in the preparation of development plans and waste disposal plans (Circular 17/91; paras 9 - 12). Local authorities are also encouraged to work with the NRA to identify suitable locations for new sewage treatment works required to improve the quality of bathing waters. Local plans and UDP Part IIs should include policies and proposals for treatment works, and proposals maps should identify the sites to which the proposals apply. These matters are considered appropriate for inclusion in waste local plans (para. 7).

Presumptions in favour of water industry proposals should be weighed differently in designated sites and areas. A threefold classification is suggested:

- the presence of a Ramsar site, or Special Protection Area for Birds, would normally outweigh water development proposals;

- SSSIs and National Nature Reserves should be avoided if at all possible; and

- special care should be exercised over the location of plant in National Parks, AONBs and the Broads (para. 18).

B4.1   CONTROL OF POLLUTION

B4.1.1   *General Policy on Pollution*

Five out of eleven plans reviewed contain a general policy on pollution, although none includes it in an initial overall County Strategy section.

Clwyd states in the Explanatory Memorandum that the original Structure Plan was amended to include such a policy: *'the need for a general policy on control of pollution is recognised by the new policy H11'.* This policy reads:

> PROPOSALS FOR DEVELOPMENT SHOULD NOT HAVE AN UNACCEPTABLE EFFECT ON HEALTH, ON THE NATURAL ENVIRONMENT OR ON GENERAL AMENITY BY EMISSIONS TO WATER, LAND OR THE ATMOSPHERE, OR BY NOISE OR VIBRATION.

The lower case justification also explains that 'acceptability' will be decided after consultations with relevant authorities, a point not always made clear in other plans.

> *Whilst it is not possible to eliminate completely all emissions of noise, dust, fumes and effluent, new developments will be expected to limit such emissions to acceptable levels. In deciding on the acceptability of a proposal the local planning authority will have regard, where appropriate, to available scientific and medical evidence and the advice of the relevant authorities for controlling pollution.*

Warwickshire's policy E12 is more elaborate, setting out particular measures which will be used to limit pollution:

> *The effects of pollution will be limited, and new sources prevented from becoming established, by measures including:*
>
> • *prohibiting further residential development within areas affected by excessive noise or atmospheric pollution from a source which cannot be abated;*
>
> • *prohibiting development, other than that required for the statutory purposes of a Water Company, adjacent to sewage treatment works or pumping stations;*
>
> • *controlling new development so as to prevent pollution of water supplies, rivers or the atmosphere; and*

Warwickshire's approved plan includes an additional measure in policy E12:

> • *prohibiting development in areas likely to be affected by landfill gas and leachate with gas producing potential.*

Nottinghamshire's policy 10/1 is a general policy for the protection and enhancement of the environment, including a sub-criterion that development proposals should avoid pollution by specific emissions; this policy was broadly acceptable (with minor modifications) to the Secretary of State.

North Yorkshire too has a general pollution policy E7 which appears to exempt important local existing industries of agriculture, mineral extraction and processing.

Lancashire's policy 69 again is different in that it aims at pollution reduction/prevention by certain actions of compliance with standards for polluting and receiving developments (see *Sections B4.1.3 and B4.1.4* below):

> ### Policy 69
>
> *To reduce pollution from any source by:*
>
> (a) *Requiring air pollution levels to comply with the air quality standards in the European Community Directive.*
>
> (b) *Refusing proposals which are likely to increase levels of pollution in watercourses and ground water to an unacceptable extent.*
>
> (c) *Securing through North West Water improvements to the quality of watercourses, estuarine and coastal waters.*
>
> (d) *Requiring appropriate sound insulation standards for new residential and community proposals in locations that are exposed to high levels of noise.*

These general policies have been set out in full to illustrate the different approaches being taken by different authorities, not necessarily only in more recent plans (for instance, Lancashire's was approved in December 1989). Those Structure Plans in this Review which do not have a general policy were all in Cross et al's Category III (ie with few pollution control policies), with the exception of Durham and Leicestershire.

Other County Statements of Policy

Many Counties are currently preparing Environmental Statements or Strategies, sometimes on the basis of Environmental Audits, which may be referred to in their Structure Plan. Leicestershire includes in its plan references to its Environmental Statement adopted in May 1989, which included a commitment to "*act and campaign against all forms of environmental pollution*". This is not a policy put forward in the Structure Plan for Secretary of State approval, but it may be that, as more Counties prepare Audits or adopt Strategies for the Environment, these will be reflected in their planning policies towards pollution.

B4.1.2   *Treatment of Pollution as a Topic*

Pollution policies are usually included in chapters on the Environment, or in specific key issue chapters on employment, housing, minerals, waste etc. It is therefore not always easy to locate such policies, nor to evaluate the relative weight given to them in the Structure Plan. Chapters on the Environment, for instance, are sometimes placed at the front (as at Leicestershire, where it forms the second chapter after the general strategy), or at the end (as at Clwyd) - but this does not necessarily indicate that the issues are more or less important.

Besides general policies towards pollution, a distinction can be made between policies towards polluting activities or developments, and policies towards other development which may be affected by those activities.

B4.1.3   *Policies on Polluting Activities*

All the Structure Plans reviewed except Warwickshire included policies on polluting activities, sometimes specifying the particular activity (such as agricultural service industries and intensive livestock units in North Yorkshire) and sometimes referring more generally to "bad neighbour development" (Kent) or general or special industrial development (Clwyd and Nottinghamshire), possibly reflecting the character of the County's employment base. For instance, Dyfed's policy EN 11 specifies that proposals for new coniferous afforestation shall minimise potential acidification of water-courses.

Some of these policies take the form of site-location policies for bad neighbour development, and others the form of more direct pollution control in requiring suitable measures to minimise emissions (as North Yorkshire's policy A4), or stating that development should not increase pollution to "unacceptable levels" (Clwyd and Cornwall).

B4.1.4   *Policies On Sensitive Developments*

Just over half the Plans reviewed had policies for the location of development in relation to existing or potentially polluting activities. Clwyd altered its original such policy in order to protect **all** forms of new development from pollution and hazard, rather than housing only as in the old policy. The new policy H13 now reads:

> *THERE WILL BE A PRESUMPTION AGAINST NEW DEVELOPMENT WHICH WOULD BE ADVERSELY AFFECTED BY WATER, AIR OR NOISE POLLUTION OR POSSIBLE HAZARD FROM INDUSTRY, QUARRYING, AND NOTIFIABLE PIPELINES.*

The reasoned justification explains that:

> *There are several large industrial concerns and working quarries within the County where problems of environmental conflict with other land uses occasionally occur. The powers available under the Control of Pollution Act, 1974, and standards enforced by the Alkali Inspectorate and Health and Safety Executive may help to minimise the problem. However, for economic and technical reasons, it is often not possible completely to eliminate a nuisance. In such cases, it is clearly desirable to minimise future nuisance by restriction on new development in severely affected areas.*

B4.1.5   *Hazardous Installations*

Some Structure Plans deal separately with hazardous installations as a form of potentially polluting activity, both in terms of policies for their development and to control developments in their vicinity. For instance, North Yorkshire include this within their general pollution control policy E7, whereas Dyfed has a specific policy E14 against "*the development of new or expansion of existing hazardous installations*", with a separate policy E15 giving a presumption against developments in their vicinity.

E

Lancashire's Policy 28 is also not to permit new development in the vicinity of installations notified as major hazards by the Health and Safety Executive, and not to permit new hazardous uses close to residential areas.

There seems therefore to be a distinction between policies which presume against any new hazardous activity, and those which presume against any near residential areas.

B4.1.6   Noise

Although this research is not specifically looking at noise as a form of pollution (where there is existing planning advice, past experience, and a draft PPG out for consultation), the Structure Plan review revealed that over half the plans did mention noise in general or activity-specific policies.

B4.1.7   Specific Areas' Protection

One point which emerged in this review is that, apart from the need for potentially polluting activities to be located away from certain sensitive developments, there were few other policies giving protection from pollution to particular areas. Only Nottinghamshire has a policy for Aquifer Protection Zones (9/5); Warwickshire's general policy E12 refers to the protection of water supplies but does not specify areas, while Clwyd moved from an earlier policy which listed areas of concern over water quality to one referring to all coastal and inland water.

Nottinghamshire's policy was modified by the Secretary of State to include reference to the NRA:

> WITHIN THE PRIORITY AQUIFER PROTECTION ZONES DEFINED BY THE NATIONAL RIVERS AUTHORITY, PERMISSION WILL NOT NORMALLY BE GRANTED WITHOUT FULL PROTECTIVE MEASURES FOR THE FOLLOWING TYPES OF DEVELOPMENT THAT CAN LEAD TO THE INFILTRATION OF HARMFUL POLLUTANTS INTO AQUIFERS FROM WHICH PUBLIC WATER SUPPLIES ARE DRAWN:
>
> (A)   WASTE DISPOSAL SITES;
> (B)   WATER RECLAMATION WORKS:
> (C)   INDUSTRIES AND AGRICULTURAL ACTIVITIES WITH PROCESSES AND/OR STORAGE INVOLVING TOXIC OR OTHERWISE HARMFUL SUBSTANCES, AS SPECIFIED BY THE APPROPRIATE GOVERNMENT DEPARTMENT OR AGENCY (INCLUDING THE NATIONAL RIVERS AUTHORITY).

B4.1.8   Policies For Consultation On Development Proposals

The Structure Plans were not reviewed for evidence of the views of consultees in the preparation of the plan (some in any case only being at Consultation Draft stage), but they were reviewed for any reference in their policies to the need to consult with the relevant pollution control authorities on particular developments. As County Councils are not development control authorities except for minerals and waste proposals, it is perhaps not surprising that there is little reference to the need to consult. Clwyd refers, in the lower-case paragraphs for policies H11 and H12 on control of pollution and quality of water, to advice and consultation with the relevant authority. Warwickshire's policy E9 includes reference to consultations on the routing of service installations such as pipelines.

In this connection, no reference was found in the explanatory justifications to the Environmental Protection legislation as a Bill or as a prospective Act, even though some of the plans were drafted in 1989/1990.

B4.2 WASTE DISPOSAL POLICIES

The treatment of waste disposal in the Structure Plans reviewed is very varied: four have separate chapters on Waste Disposal, four contain waste disposal policies in their Environment/Urban and Rural Conservation Chapters, and two have joint Minerals and Waste Disposal Chapters. In Wales, waste disposal is a District matter, but both Clwyd and Dyfed include policies on waste in their Environment chapters.

B4.2.1 General Waste Disposal Policies

Three of the Structure Plans favour a particular route for disposal: Dyfed and Norfolk favour landfill (in their policies EN22 and WD1), while Nottinghamshire's Structure Plan contains a County Council commitment (not for Secretary of State approval) to incineration for the disposal of waste.

B4.2.2 Criteria For Assessing Waste Disposal Site Proposals

The Structure Plans' criteria for suitable sites for waste disposal vary from Durham's Policy 116, giving very general criteria of economic and environmental suitability, to Lancashire's policy 106 which details criteria on traffic, agricultural land, landscape, and built and natural environment. Norfolk's draft policy WD3 gives clear criteria for assessing proposals, including one on the record of the operator.

IN CONSIDERING ALL PROPOSALS FOR DEALING WITH WASTE INCLUDING LANDFILL AND OTHER TREATMENT AND DISPOSAL METHODS THE COUNTY COUNCIL WILL HAVE REGARD TO THE FOLLOWING FACTORS WHERE APPROPRIATE:

(I)   THE NEED FOR WASTE DISPOSAL FACILITIES IN THE CONTEXT OF THE STRATEGY CONTAINED IN THE WASTE DISPOSAL PLAN;

(II)   THE IMPACT OF THE OPERATION AND THE FINAL LANDFORM ON THE LANDSCAPE, PARTICULARLY IN OR ADJACENT TO AREAS OF OUTSTANDING NATURAL BEAUTY, RIVER VALLEYS AND THE BROADS AUTHORITY AREA;

(III)   THE EFFECT OF ALL WASTE DISPOSAL OPERATIONS AND FACILITIES ON THE ENVIRONMENT, RESIDENTIAL AND VISUAL AMENITIES, AIR QUALITY AND NOISE LEVELS;

(IV)   THE EFFECT ON WATER RESOURCES, LAND DRAINAGE, RIVERS AND WATER COURSES;

(V)   THE IMPACT OF LORRY AND OTHER VEHICLE TRAFFIC ON THE HIGHWAY NETWORK AND LOCAL RESIDENTIAL AND OTHER AMENITIES;

(VI)   *THE LOSS OF GOOD QUALITY AGRICULTURAL LAND (GRADES 1, 2 AND 3A);*

(VII)   *THE DAMAGE TO AREAS OF ARCHAEOLOGICAL, SCIENTIFIC OR NATURE CONSERVATION INTEREST;*

(VIII)   *POTENTIAL BIRD STRIKE HAZARD CLOSE TO AIRFIELDS;*

(IX)   *STERILIZATION OF MINERAL DEPOSITS;*

(X)   *THE IMPACT OF GAS GENERATION ON SURROUNDING VEGETATION AND PROPERTIES;*

(XI)   *THE SCOPE FOR SATISFACTORY AND VIABLE RESTORATION OF THE LAND TO A DESIRABLE AFTER USE;*

(XII)   *THE BENEFIT OF RESTORING WORKED OUT DERELICT MINERAL WORKING AS OPPOSED TO LAND RAISING ON GREENFIELD SITES; AND*

(XIII)   *THE APPLICANT'S RECORD OF WORKING AND RESTORING SITES.*

B4.2.3   *Policies for Control of Waste Disposal Sites*

Norfolk also includes a draft policy WD4 setting out the matters which conditions on any planning consent or site licence might cover:

THE COUNTY COUNCIL WILL, WHERE APPROPRIATE, SEEK TO SECURE, EITHER BY CONDITIONS ATTACHED TO THE PLANNING PERMISSION, THE SITE LICENCE OR BY VOLUNTARY AGREEMENT:

(I)   *APPROPRIATE CATEGORIES OF WASTE TO BE DISPOSED IN THE PARTICULAR LOCATION;*

(II)   *A PROGRAMME SETTING OUT THE METHOD, PHASING AND COMPLETION OF WASTE DISPOSAL INCLUDING THE SPECIFICATION OF THE TYPE AND METHOD OF FILLING TO ENSURE THAT THE RESTORED AREA MEETS THE REQUIREMENTS OF THE PLANNED AFTER-USE INCLUDING MEASURES TO DEAL WITH LEACHATE AND LANDFILL GAS WHERE NECESSARY;*

(III)   *RESTORATION OF THE LAND TO A CONDITION AND LANDFORM SUITABLE FOR AN APPROPRIATE AFTER-USE, SUCH AS AGRICULTURE, FORESTRY, RECREATION, NATURE CONSERVATION OR OTHER FORMS OF DEVELOPMENT COMPATIBLE WITH GOVERNMENT LEGISLATION AND ADVICE AND STRUCTURE AND LOCAL PLAN POLICIES AND EMBODYING THE LATEST ADVANCES IN SAFETY POLICIES AND RESTORATION TECHNIQUES, THE DEVELOPMENT OF WHICH THE COUNTY COUNCIL WILL ENCOURAGE;*

(IV)   *THE AFTERCARE OF RESTORED LAND TO A STANDARD FIT FOR SUBSEQUENT USE OF AGRICULTURE, FORESTRY OR AMENITY, WHERE APPROPRIATE;*

(V)   *SUCH PROVISIONS, INCLUDING LANDSCAPING, AS ARE REQUIRED TO PROTECT THE AMENITY OF THE AREA DURING AND AFTER WORKING;*

(VI)   *SUCH PROVISIONS AS ARE REQUIRED TO PROTECT WATER RESOURCES, LAND DRAINAGE, NATURE CONSERVATION INTERESTS AND HIGHWAY CONSIDERATIONS;*

(VII)   *THE INVESTIGATION OF SITES OF ARCHAEOLOGICAL INTEREST AND THE RECOVERY OF ARCHAEOLOGICAL ARTEFACTS FROM SUCH SITES;*

(VIII)   WHERE APPROPRIATE AND PRACTICABLE, THE ROUTING OF TRAFFIC TO AND
FROM THE SITE;

(IX)   THE UPGRADING OF DAMAGED LAND IN THE APPLICANT'S CONTROL OR
OWNERSHIP WHERE APPROPRIATE AND BY AGREEMENT;

(X)   THE BENEFIT OF PLANNING PERMISSION SOLELY TO THE OPERATING
COMPANY WHERE PARTICULAR ISSUES SUCH AS THE COMPANY'S
RECORD OR CIRCUMSTANCES HAVE BEEN MATERIAL FACTORS IN
GRANTING A PERMISSION.

B4.2.4   Restoration and After-Care

All the structure plans reviewed contain policies requiring restoration, with
some also requiring proposals for after-care for an appropriate period, such
as Leicestershire's draft MWDP3:

> When granting planning permission for mineral working or the use of land for the disposal of waste
> materials or related development, the County Council will require restoration to an acceptable use at
> the earliest opportunity. After restoration has been completed the County Council will require a
> programme of aftercare for an appropriate period. The best and most versatile agricultural land will
> normally be restored to an agricultural use. On other land, priority will normally be given to
> restoration to water recreation, forestry or nature conservation.

B4.2.5   Waste Minimisation

Some of the Structure Plans reviewed have policies to promote recycling,
waste minimisation or the need for reduction in land-take for disposal or
treatment. Norfolk's policy WD1 encourages recycling, while lower-case
policy WD1a refers to support for, inter alia, waste reduction.

B4.2.6   Reference To Waste Disposal Plans

Few of the structure plans reviewed refer to a Waste Disposal Plan prepared
under the Control of Pollution Act, and it is therefore difficult to assess the
extent to which they have been taken into account, if indeed they exist, in
the preparation of the development plan. Norfolk does refer to its Waste
Disposal Plan in Policy WD3, which might explain the inclusion of a full
policy WD4 on planning conditions, site licensing and agreements, quoted in
full above.

Leicestershire refers to its approved Waste Disposal Plan, and to the
requirement to prepare a Waste Disposal Development Plan, but includes
few waste policies in its draft structure plan.

B5.1   CONTROL OF POLLUTION

B5.1.1   *General Policy on Pollution*

Five out of the seven UDPs reviewed contain a general policy towards pollution. Wakefield, Sheffield, Bexley and Wigan give such policies "Part 1" status, but only Sheffield includes such a policy in its overall Strategic Policy SP1d.

The policy states:

SP1 Strategic Policy

The UDP will help to manage future change and growth in Sheffield. It aims to achieve a balance between competing land uses, new development, conservation, and integrated transport provision. In this way, it will contribute to the social, economic and environmental regeneration of Sheffield by:....

(d) reducing all forms of pollution and improving the quality of the environment.

Wigan's policies EN1 and EN3 are:

EN1 ENVIRONMENTAL PROTECTION AND ENHANCEMENT:

THE COUNCIL WILL SEEK TO PROTECT AND ENHANCE THE CHARACTER AND APPEARANCE OF THE ENVIRONMENT BY:

(A)   PROTECTING AND ENHANCING THE FABRIC AND APPEARANCE OF THE ENVIRONMENT AND OF THE BOROUGH'S HERITAGE;

(B)   PROTECTING AND IMPROVING SEMI-NATURAL HABITATS AND LANDSCAPES;

(C)   CONTROLLING POLLUTION, DANGERS AND EYESORES.

EN3 POLLUTION:

THE COUNCIL WILL SEEK TO REDUCE POLLUTION BY:

(A)   NOT PERMITTING DEVELOPMENT WHICH IS LIKELY TO RESULT IN UNACCEPTABLE LEVELS OF AIR POLLUTION, NOR WHICH WOULD BE LIKELY TO PREJUDICE THE USE OF ADJACENT LAND RESERVED FOR OTHER USES;

(B)   NOT PERMITTING DEVELOPMENT WHICH IS LIKELY TO RESULT IN UNACCEPTABLE LEVELS OF POLLUTION IN WATERCOURSES AND GROUND WATER;

(C)   NOT PERMITTING DEVELOPMENT WHICH IS LIKELY TO RESULT IN UNACCEPTABLE LEVELS OF NOISE IN PROXIMITY TO DWELLINGS OR COMMUNITY USES, NOR WHICH WOULD BE LIKELY TO PREJUDICE THE USE OF LAND RESERVED FOR OTHER USES.

Newcastle's policy NC6 for the control of pollution in relation to wildlife is *'thought necessary to underline that wildlife can be adversely affected by levels of pollution much lower or more localised than would affect human health'* (paragraph 3.112)

B5.1.2 *Treatment of Pollution as a Topic*

Five of the plans include pollution policies in their chapters on the Environment, to which Wakefield gives key place after its overall policy of regeneration. Sheffield has a separate chapter on Pollution and Waste.

B5.1.3 *Policies on Polluting Activities*

As UDPs contain both Part 1 (strategic) and Part 2 (local) policies, it might be expected that they would include detailed policies for particular activities or developments. Bexley, for instance, has policies dealing with the potentially polluting effects (smells and fumes) of non-retail central area uses (policy SHO 6), as well as a more general policy ENV 30 requiring all developments to be assessed against a criterion of unreasonable emissions, and an employment policy E1 for industrial and commercial activity referring to discharges.

Coventry, Wigan and Sheffield have policies for special industrial uses.

B5.1.4 *Policy on Sensitive Developments*

Four of the seven plans include policies for the location of development in relation to polluting activities. Bexley (ENV 30) and Coventry (BE 17) have policies that development may be restricted in areas subject to pollution or potential pollution, while Sheffield (IB 19) and Wakefield (E 50) require a buffer zone or break between heavy industry and sensitive uses (Sheffield) or potentially hazardous industry and housing (Wakefield). Sheffield defines sensitive uses to include *'hotels and hostels (C1), residential institutions (C2), houses (C3), community facilities (D1) and leisure and recreation facilities (D2)'*. Sheffield also reinforces this with policies PW1 on air pollution and sensitive uses, PW2 on noise pollution and sensitive uses, H13e on housing and residential institutions, and PW6 on the need for development for housing, education and employment uses to avoid high voltage power lines. This array of policies follows:

PW1 AIR POLLUTION

THE CITY COUNCIL WILL USE ALL ITS AVAILABLE POWERS AND INFLUENCE TO PREVENT OR MINIMISE AIR POLLUTION.

PLANNING PERMISSION WILL NOT NORMALLY BE GRANTED FOR DEVELOPMENTS WHICH WOULD:

(A)   CREATE SIGNIFICANT AIR POLLUTION; OR
(B)   LOCATE SENSITIVE USES AND SOURCES OF AIR POLLUTION CLOSE TOGETHER.

IB19 SITING HEAVY INDUSTRIES AND SENSITIVE USES NEAR TO EACH OTHER:

AN ENVIRONMENTAL BUFFER WILL BE REQUIRED BETWEEN HEAVY INDUSTRY AND SENSITIVE USES.

H13 CONDITIONS FOR DEVELOPMENT IN HOUSING AREAS

WITHIN HOUSING AREAS PLANNING PERMISSION FOR DEVELOPMENT WILL NORMALLY BE GRANTED PROVIDED THAT ....

(E) THE SITE IS NOT AFFECTED BY AIR POLLUTION, NOISE OR OTHER NUISANCE OR RISK TO PUBLIC HEALTH AND/OR SAFETY.

PW6 HIGH-VOLTAGE POWER LINES

BUILDING WILL NORMALLY NOT BE PERMITTED DIRECTLY BENEATH HIGH-VOLTAGE POWER LINES, AND DEVELOPMENT FOR HOUSING, EDUCATION AND EMPLOYMENT USES, IN PARTICULAR, WILL BE DISCOURAGED WITHIN 50 METRES.

B5.1.5   *Hazardous Installations and Processes*

Some such policies have been noted in *Section B4.1.4* above, but only Tower Hamlets has specific Employment policies 25-27 on Hazardous Development and the Storage of Hazardous Materials:

EMPL25 PROPOSALS FOR NEW DEVELOPMENT, RE-DEVELOPMENT OR AN INTENSIFICATION OF AN EXISTING USE WHICH INVOLVES THE STORAGE OR USE OF LARGE QUANTITIES OF HAZARDOUS PRODUCTS WILL BE RESISTED, SIMILAR PROPOSALS IN NEIGHBOURING BOROUGHS MAY ALSO BE OPPOSED.

EMPL26 CONDITIONS WILL BE IMPOSED ON CONSENTS FOR NEW DEVELOPMENT OF WHATEVER KIND ARISING OUT OF THE ADVICE GIVEN BY THE HEALTH AND SAFETY EXECUTIVE, IN ORDER TO LIMIT THE RISKS ASSOCIATED WITH THE STORAGE OF HAZARDOUS MATERIALS.

EMPL27 CONSULTATION AND LIAISON WILL BE UNDERTAKEN WITH THE HEALTH AND SAFETY EXECUTIVE ON ANY SIGNIFICANT DEVELOPMENT INVOLVING OR LIKELY TO BE AFFECTED BY HAZARDOUS PRODUCTS OR PROCESSES.

B5.1.6   *Noise*

As with the equivalent structure plan policies, many general pollution policies in UDPs include reference to noise, and some detailed development control policies also (for instance, in Bexley, policies on house-conversions, air-traffic, hotels and late-night uses). Sheffield's draft UDP includes a specific policy PW2 on Noise Pollution equivalent to that on Air Pollution:

PW2 NOISE POLLUTION

THE CITY COUNCIL WILL USE ALL ITS AVAILABLE POWERS AND INFLUENCE TO PREVENT OR MINIMISE NOISE POLLUTION.

PLANNING PERMISSION WILL NOT NORMALLY BE GRANTED FOR DEVELOPMENTS WHICH WOULD:

(A)   CREATE NOISE LEVELS IN EXCESS OF LEGAL LIMITS; OR

(B)   LOCATE SENSITIVE USES AND SOURCES OF NOISE POLLUTION CLOSE TOGETHER.

Tower Hamlets and Bexley both include detailed standards for sound insulation and noise.

B5.1.7 *Protected Areas*

The main concern of the UDPs reviewed in terms of protecting particular areas is to improve the quality of watercourses: Tower Hamlets' OS21(2), Newcastle's NC7, and Sheffield's PW5 all have this objective, while Wakefield's policy OL6 for the protection of flood washlands refers to the serious risk **to** development in these areas from pollution.

B5.1.8 *Policies for Consultation on Development Proposals*

The UDPs treat this matter in different ways: Tower Hamlets' policy EMP27 on hazardous substances or processes makes consultation with the Health and Safety Executive part of the policy, and Coventry in E20 refers to the need for advice on proposals for special industrial uses:

E20: SPECIAL INDUSTRIAL USES

PROPOSALS FOR SPECIAL INDUSTRIAL USES (USE CLASSES B3-B7) WILL BE DETERMINED IN THE LIGHT OF THE FOLLOWING CONSIDERATIONS:

(I)   THE ADVICE OF THE POLLUTION INSPECTORATE AND THE DIRECTOR OF ENVIRONMENTAL SERVICES, COVENTRY CITY COUNCIL.

(II)   THE ABILITY OF THE OPERATOR TO SATISFY THE CITY COUNCIL IN RESPECT OF VISUAL AMENITY, POLLUTION CONTROL MEASURES IN TERMS OF NOISE, AIR AND WATER, AND THE ABILITY TO REDUCE, TO ACCEPTABLE LEVELS, ANY ADVERSE IMPACT ON THE AMENITIES OF NEARBY OCCUPIERS.

(III) THE HIGHWAY AND GENERAL SAFETY IMPLICATIONS OF THE MOVEMENT OF GOODS AND RAW MATERIALS IN AND OUT OF THE SITE.

ENVIRONMENTAL ASSESSMENT MAY BE REQUIRED.

Sheffield and Wakefield include statements about consultation with HMIP and NRA in lower case policy justification paragraphs, in Sheffield's case headed *'How it will be put into practice'*:

Monitoring air quality against statutory and other accepted standards in order to measure the nature and extent of pollution.

Monitoring progress made in implementing measures to improve air quality.

Regulating existing air polluting activities in accordance with statutory requirements.

Liaising with other air pollution control agencies (eg Her Majesty's Inspectorate of Pollution) on polluting activities outside the City Council's powers.

Carrying out extensive consultations with pollution control agencies (eg Health and Consumer Services Department and Her Majesty's Inspectorate of Pollution) before determining planning applications.

B5.1.9   *Reference to Environmental Protection Act*

Despite the fact that UDPs are of recent preparation, it seems that none refers to the Environmental Protection Act, although Wakefield refers, at paragraph 10.5.44, to legislative changes affecting waste.

B5.2   *WASTE DISPOSAL POLICIES*

As with the structure plans reviewed, the treatment of waste as a topic in these UDPs varies considerably: three have separate chapters on waste, one a chapter on pollution and waste, with the others treating it in chapters on Public Utilities (Tower Hamlets), Social and Community Facilities (Coventry), and Open Land (Wakefield). The extent to which the UDPs incorporate the equivalent of a Waste Local Plan is not made clear.

B5.2.1   *General Waste Disposal Policies*

It might be expected that urban areas would have policies to reflect the amount of waste generated and the lack of voids, and a number of authorities do indicate that capacity needs to be found for treatment or disposing of waste generated within their area (such as Sheffield's PW8). Coventry includes a policy SC22 favouring incineration, while Wakefield in OL11 favours landfill *'until such time as better or more appropriate waste disposal options become available.'*

B5.2.2   *Criteria for Assessing Waste Treatment or Disposal Sites*

Most of the UDPs include policies for the assessment of such developments, with some having separate policies for Civic Amenity (Coventry SC24) or Dumping Sites (Sheffield PW10). Bexley has a policy against further Waste Transfer Stations in residential areas (WAS1). Tower Hamlets policy U9 states that new Waste Transfer Stations will have to comply with Planning Standard No 11, which is set out in a separate volume of the UDP.

Wakefield's policy OL12 sets out general criteria for assessing proposals, while Wigan in policy WD1D lists 8 criteria:

Assessing Waste Disposal Proposals

Proposals for waste disposal will normally be permitted only when the following criteria are satisfied:

(a) It will not have an unacceptable impact on dwellings or on other environmentally sensitive properties in terms of visual amenity, noise, vibration, dust, smells, litter, vermin, air pollution, water pollution, landfill gas migration or other nuisance.

(b) It will not have an unacceptable adverse effect on land drainage and water supply.

(c) The access arrangements are satisfactory and traffic generated will not have an unacceptable effect on properties adjoining routes used by site traffic or on road safety anywhere between the site and the strategic highway network.

(d) It will not have an unacceptable effect on the viability of agricultural holdings or lead to an unacceptable loss of agricultural land, taking into account the quality of restoration likely to be achieved following waste disposal.

(e) It will not have an unacceptable effect on the setting of buildings of architectural or historic interest, ancient monuments or conservation areas.

(f) Local features of landscape, ecological, archaeological or geological interest within the site or locality are protected as far as possible.

(g) It will not have an unacceptable impact on areas of recreational use or potential, the Douglas Valley or areas of ecological importance.

(h) There is a satisfactory scheme of screening, landscaping and restoration.

B5.2.3   *Policies for Control of Waste Disposal Sites*

As with the structure plans, some authorities include policies for the control of waste sites through conditions or agreements. Wakefield states in policy OL13 that acceptable proposals will be subject to conditions and agreements, while Wigan includes a similar Part 2 policy WD1E:

Control of Waste Disposal:

Where waste disposal is acceptable in principle, the Council will as appropriate:

(a) limit the period of operations;
(b) control levels of noise;
(c) control hours of working and maintenance;
(d) ensure satisfactory access to the site;
(e) prevent or control the production of polluted water, smells, wind-blown litter and dust;
(f) ensure steps are taken to monitor and control landfill gas and leachate which may be produced by the site once the development is completed;
(g) limit the visual impact of the development;
(h) ensure that the site is satisfactorily restored, preferably with a scheme of phased working and restoration in appropriate cases;
(i) ensure that suitable provisions for aftercare are made in the case of restoration to agriculture, forestry or amenity use.

B5.2.4   *Recycling and Waste Minimisation*

Newcastle, Sheffield, Wigan and Coventry all have policies promoting or encouraging the recycling of waste. Recycling centres in general are treated as waste transfer stations, and subject to the general locational criteria for waste sites or, in Wigan, the criteria for special industrial uses set out in policy E1D. Sheffield refers to a policy in its separate Waste Management Plan (see Section C4-2-6 below) to promote waste reduction. Wigan is the only authority to include a policy stating that waste disposal arrangements should be considered when a major project is proposed as indicated by Part 2 policy WD1A.

WD1A   Building and Construction Wastes

The council will consider proposals for the disposal of building and construction wastes against the criteria in policy WD1D. In the case of major building and civil engineering projects, it will give full consideration to the disposal of any waste arising at the time that permission is sought for the project itself.

Building, construction and civil engineering activities may all generate considerable amounts of waste material for disposal. Although such proposals will be assessed in the normal way against the criteria laid down in Policy WD1D, it is important, particularly with the larger projects, to consider the disposal arrangements at the outset. The council will, therefore, expect waste disposal arrangements to be considered when application for a major project is made so that the full implications of the proposal can be considered.

B5.2.5 *Restoration and After-care*

Those authorities contemplating landfill also have policies requiring the submission of schemes for satisfactory restoration and after-care, such as Coventry's SC23 landfill policy and Wigan's policy WD1D for assessing waste disposal proposals and WD1E for controlling them.

Wigan also has a policy encouraging the re-use of landfill gas (WD2B), and Coventry has a policy on the risks of landfill gas from active and closed landfill sites (BE21).

B5.2.6 *Reference to Waste Disposal Plans*

The position is more complicated than with County Councils, which were responsible for the production of Waste Disposal Plans under COPA. Unitary Authorities operate under a variety of regimes. Neither of the London UDPs refers to the London Waste Regulation Authority. Wigan refers to the Greater Manchester WDP as in preparation, but has also itself prepared a WDP (p 111). Sheffield has a Waste Management Plan (p322), while Wakefield and Newcastle refer to their respective former Metropolitan County WDP (West Yorkshire, and Tyne and Wear). Newcastle is the only authority to refer to the WDP in a policy (WD1).

B5.3 ENVIRONMENTAL ASSESSMENT

Three of the UDPs (Sheffield, Wakefield, and Coventry) include specific policies requiring submission of Environmental Statements for major developments as appropriate within the context of the 1988 Regulations. Bexley's policy WAS3 requires an EA, where appropriate, for proposals for waste processing, including an assessment of any cumulative effects.

B6.1   CONTROL OF POLLUTION

B6.1.1   **General Policy on Pollution**

Three of the local plans reviewed contain a general policy on pollution;
Torfaen includes pollution as an issue for consideration in its general
development policy P/G1:

P/G1

The Borough Council will aim to ensure that all new development is in accordance with the policies
and proposals in the Local Plan. In general all proposals must be satisfactory when considered
against the following criteria:

D. The impact of the proposal upon the environment. In particular the following issues will be
carefully considered:

1. *Pollution*
2. *Existing Landscape and Natural Features*
3. *Existing Topography*
4. *Features of Historic/Archaeological Interest*
5. *Agricultural Interests*
6. *Nature Conservation Interests*

Copeland's policy ENV 24 is unique in amongst those examined that the
Council will maintain a register of pollution:

The Council will maintain a register of pollution based on existing data supplemented by its own
monitoring programme and it will support environmental monitoring and analysis by others where
this leads to greater knowledge of the local environment.

B6.1.2   **Policies on Polluting Activities**

More of the local plans have specific policies on the impact of polluting
activities in relation to nearby residential and other uses. Crawley in policy
GD10 will *'take account of'* the proposed location of any potentially polluting
activity in relation to other development. Copeland's policy EMP17(a) refers
to *'no unreasonable disturbance to the locality being created'*, whereas
Woodspring's policy CNP/ENV6 gives a more negative presumption.
Copeland and Warrington both have policies for buffer zones for certain
industrial development. Warrington's policy reads:

ENV.17 - INDUSTRIAL DEVELOPMENT GUIDELINES

THE COUNCIL WILL EXPECT A HIGH STANDARD OF INDUSTRIAL DEVELOPMENT
AND WILL REQUIRE THAT ALL DEVELOPMENT PROPOSALS CONFORM TO THE
GUIDANCE OUTLINED BELOW AND THE COUNCIL'S ADOPTED STANDARDS...

VII)   FOR INDUSTRIAL SITES IN CLOSE PROXIMITY TO HOUSING OR RECREATION
USES, LANDSCAPED 'BUFFER ZONES' SHOULD BE PROVIDED ALONG THEIR
MORE SENSITIVE BOUNDARIES AND CONSIDERATION GIVEN TO THE USE OF

*OTHER MEASURES SUCH AS SOUND INSULATION, POLLUTION CONTROL
AND RESTRICTED HOURS OF WORKING TO MINIMISE POTENTIAL AMENITY
PROBLEMS.*

B6.1.3   *Policy on Sensitive Developments*

Fewer of the local plans reviewed have the obverse of the above policies in
determining proposals for the location of sensitive development. Crawley's
GD11 and Woodspring's CNP/ENV4 and CNP/ENV7 do so. Copeland also
has a policy for a programme of smoke control (ENV25).

Woodspring's policy CNP/ENV7 on the location of sensitive development in
relation to sources of atmospheric pollution is:

> *Development normally will not be permitted where the emission of grit, dust, smoke, smuts, fumes,
> effluvia or odours is in the opinion of the District Council likely to interfere with the enjoyment of
> the proposed development.*

B6.1.4   *Hazardous Installations and Processes*

Woodspring and Copeland both have full policies for Hazardous Installations
and Substances, Copeland's covering nuclear reactors and reprocessing plant
at Sellafield, and chemical plant on the coast.

B6.1.5   *Noise*

The more traditional concerns of LPAs with noise control are reflected in the
wider range of policies for the control of noise. Copeland, Woodspring and
Forest Heath have separate policies for noise, and both Forest Heath and
Crawley have specific policies for airport noise, and for housing
developments in relation to noise from those locations. Woodspring also has
separate policies for vibration.

B6.1.6   *Protected Areas*

Woodspring's local plan is the only one reviewed to specify particular areas
for protection from pollution: CNP/ENV 10iii gives protection to *'any
watercourse, pond, stream, sea or other area of water'*.

B6.1.7   *Policies for Consultations on Development Proposals*

Woodspring and Copeland, refer to the need for consultation with
appropriate agencies. Woodspring states its commitment to consultation in
lower-case explanation for its policies on Atmospheric Pollution and Water
Pollution. Copeland makes provision for consultation part of its policies on
aerial and liquid discharges, and is the only authority to make clear reference
(in paragraph 9.7.2) to the Environmental Protection Act 1990 and the
responsibilities of HMIP and NRA.

District Councils in England are not responsible for land-use planning functions for waste disposal, and therefore policies on this topic in District Local Plans are the exception. However Glanford, Copeland, and South Staffordshire all have paragraphs on waste disposal, with policies to indicate their likely response when consulted on waste disposal proposals.

Copelands's policies are as follows:

Policy Env 17   *The Council will actively support environmental improvements to land within the Whitehaven Urban Fringe Park and to other areas of untidy and underused land elsewhere in the urban areas of the Borough.*

Policy Env 18   *Cumbria County Council is urged to develop waste disposal options including proposals for recycling which will cause the least possible environmental damage.*

Policy Env 19   *Cumbria County Council is urged to make provision for a manned civic amenity site in Whitehaven incorporating collection points for materials suitable for recycling.*

Policy Env 20   *The Council in association with Cumbria County Council, voluntary groups and the private sector will develop a recycling strategy. Subject to appropriate siting the Council will support proposals for the collection and sorting of bottles, paper, aluminium, plastics, oil and other recyclable materials.*

Policy Env 21   *The Council will only support proposals for tipping of inert material in circumstances where there is no adverse impact on landscape or nature conservation interests and where there is good access from the main road network and where satisfactory arrangements are made for subsequent landscaping and after-use.*

The reasoned justification for policy ENV20 states:

As refuse collection authority Copeland Borough Council also has a role to play in developing policies for the segregation of recyclable wastes at source and in either the direct provision of facilities such as bottle banks or the support and promotion of initiatives in the private and voluntary sectors.

South Staffordshire explains its inclusion of waste policies in the following terms:

9.14   *While recognising that the County Council is responsible for waste disposal, the District Council considers that it is important to protect the environment and the amenity of local residents and that such local matters should be taken into account when determining development proposals for waste disposal. Any permission which is granted for the establishment of a waste disposal site should ensure that the effects on the amenity of local residents and on the environment and wildlife habitats are kept to a minimum, that the disposal of waste is strictly controlled and that sites are properly restored to an appropriate after-use. As with mineral extraction, the restoration of waste disposal sites can provide opportunities for creative after-use to benefit landscape, wildlife and recreation. Imaginative restoration proposals for such uses will be encouraged by the District Council.*

Torfaen, as a Welsh District Council with responsibility for waste collection, disposal and regulation, has prepared a Waste Disposal Plan, but includes no specific policies for waste in its draft local plan.

THE TREATMENT OF POLLUTION AND WASTE IN DEVELOPMENT PLANS

This section draws together the key issues from the review of development plans, and from the interviews, in order to address the question posed in the research brief: How have planning authorities taken account of pollution and waste management issues in development plans and how have waste disposal plans been considered?

B7.1   *A PLAN-LED PLANNING SYSTEM*

Under the new development plans regime, with the requirement in the 1991 Act that planning decisions accord with the development plans unless material considerations indicate otherwise, the status of policies will be enhanced. The Regulations also require authorities to have regard to environmental considerations in preparing their general policies and proposals in structure plans and UDP Part 1s.

Regions same!

At the same time, authorities are being encouraged to formulate policies for the whole of their areas, and Counties are empowered to adopt structure plans without referring them to the Secretary of State. It is likely that LPAs will therefore wish to respond to the concerns of residents that these planning policies serve to protect their interests, their health and their local environment. This may mean the inclusion of more pollution policies.

This enhanced status and range of policies in development plans may, however, run counter to the government's exhortation to limit the bulk and detail of plans.

B7.2   *PLANNING GUIDANCE*

The existing guidance on treatment of issues in development plans was dispersed and fragmentary until issue of the new PPG12. Otherwise issues of pollution and waste management are only addressed peripherally (eg. in minerals advice) and there is more guidance relating to waste management. In general, policy advice reflects *ad hoc* concerns (eg. landfill gas, cessation of sludge dumping in the North Sea). The advice in Waste Management Papers is often fuller than that in planning guidance. There is a need to advise on the relationship between planning and waste licensing processes and to further clarify the scope of waste local plans and potential overlaps with waste disposal plans. The advice in Regional Guidance is generally of little significance.

B7.3 ENVIRONMENTAL STRATEGIES

A number of authorities interviewed or whose plan was reviewed refer to current or proposed work towards the adoption of an Environmental Strategy for the authority's area, sometimes, as in Avon, the result of an Audit, sometimes, as in New Forest 2000, in response to particular pressures. Nottinghamshire and Leicestershire both refer to County Council policies or statements in their Structure Plans. These do not form part of the statutory development plan, but are likely to generate further pressure to include policies in development plans to implement the strategy, including policies for pollution control. (A recent study by Heriot-Watt University (1992) suggests that a high proportion of LAs are preparing or about to prepare such an audit or strategy).

B7.4 NUMBER OF POLLUTION POLICIES

This review has not systematically compared existing development plans with earlier ones for their pollution policy content, but it does seem there is an increase in the number of pollution policies: Avon and Gwent at interview indicated that their new structure plans would have more such policies, and a high proportion of the UDPs reviewed do so.

B7.5 DEFINITION OF UNACCEPTABLE POLLUTION

The policies relating to pollution range from those which presume against any development likely to cause pollution, to those which presume against development causing unacceptable levels of pollution. The question of who should decide what constitutes acceptable levels, whose advice should be taken, or what information would be required to judge this is not addressed. The planning definition may not be the same as the pollution control agencies', but the interviews suggest that the LA elected members usually wish to adopt a precautionary approach. (See also *Section B7.8* below).

B7.6 POLLUTION AS A STRATEGIC ISSUE

Many of the plans have an overall 'quality of life' theme as their dominant aim, although few at present include pollution policies as part of their overall strategy. Bexley and Sheffield are amongst those that do.

B7.7 TYPES OF POLLUTANTS

Planning policies have traditionally encompassed emissions such as noise, dust and fumes (often the concerns of Local Authority Environmental Health Departments), but are now becoming either more wide-ranging (such as policies on all emissions to air) or extending the list of possible pollutants to include, for instance, leachate and migrating gas.

F

The review of plans revealed a large number of policies relating to both polluting or potentially polluting activities and to sensitive developments. Policies relate to both existing and new development. Sometimes they take the form of traditional locational policies (allocating certain uses to certain areas, such as Special Industrial Areas), or the obverse, restricting new development near such uses or possible uses. Many of the plans still treat residential development in particular (for instance, the use classes specified by Sheffield) as sensitive development, but Clwyd's new plan protects all development, not just housing.

The planning system has experience of such locational policies, sometimes formalised as in buffer zones for noise or hazardous development, and many plans include such policies. What appears to be changing is that a narrower concern with geographically-limited emissions amenable to noise or hazard protection zones is giving way to a broader concern with other types of emissions where different policies are required. This may explain the incidence of all-encompassing pollution prevention policies, and the concern with protecting watercourses or groundwater.

B7.9   CONSULTATION IN PLAN MAKING

The evidence from the interviews was that the involvement of the pollution control agencies in development plan formulation had been minimal, despite consultation.

B7.10   POLICIES ON CONSULTATION

Statements in policies or their supporting justification on consultation with the agencies on development proposals are scanty, although the situation was evolving rapidly during the time in which some of the plans were being prepared. Only the Copeland Local Plan attempts to summarise the new situation under the Environmental Protection Act.

Plans do not discuss the expected level or quality of response, the precise contribution to decision-making to be left to the consultee.

B7.11   WASTE POLICIES

The complex of different regimes under which the plans reviewed were prepared - authorities with and without waste disposal powers, authorities with and without a waste disposal or management plan, or a waste local plan - makes it difficult to generalise about development plan policies for waste. The lack of consistency was confirmed by the interviews.

Nevertheless, many plans do contain policies for waste disposal, including those prepared by LPAs which are not responsible for waste.

B7.12   DEFINITION OF WASTE

One area of concern expressed was the definition of waste in planning waste disposal and treatment sites; for instance, whether scrap-yards or waste water treatment works constitute waste sites. This may determine which tier of LA deals with them, and hence in which development plan policies are included.

B7.13   CRITERIA FOR WASTE SITES

Sites for waste treatment or disposal are often locally controversial, an issue becoming more acute as voids fill up, and many authorities include criteria-based policies for determining proposals (such as in Norfolk), rather than specifying sites. This to some extent blurs the distinction between structure and local plan policies for waste. With the separation of waste regulation and waste disposal responsibilities under the Environmental Protection Act, the need for polices giving clear guidance to waste contractors is considered to be more important than before.

Few of the plans reviewed include particular policies for the incineration of waste, although a number state in their explanatory paragraphs that the scope for the treatment of waste by incineration will be kept under review. Some authorities still promote landfill as a means to land-reclamation, while others link the need to reduce demand for landfill sites with proposals for energy generation from incineration.

B7.14   CONDITIONS AND AGREEMENTS - POLLUTION AND WASTE

Many authorities include policies specifying the matters affecting the operation of waste sites and post-closure measures which will be the subject of conditions for planning permission, site-licence, or agreement. There are some examples of similar policies for polluting developments generally. The scope for agreements is not usually addressed separately, although they may particularly apply to gas monitoring and restoration works.

B7.15   INTEGRATED WASTE MANAGEMENT

In general, authorities seem to be moving towards a system of integrated waste management, where their development plan policies for waste need to be seen in a broader context of the authority's overall approach to waste generation, waste minimisation, recycling and alternative methods of disposal.

B7.16   CUMULATIVE IMPACTS

There are few explicit policies on cumulative impacts, but it is clear from the interviews that authorities are beginning to consider this issue, especially where the development plan contains a general pollution prevention policy.

B7.17   CONCLUSION

The incidence of pollution policies in development plans is increasing, as authorities adopt a more systematic approach than traditional concerns with 'amenity', and look to pollution prevention as a major strand in environmental policy.

While most policies seem to be in response to this broader definition of the environment, and are not explicitly based on principles, Wakefield does refer to the importance of protecting the environment through the development control process in line with the principles of full information, the polluter pays, and a preventive and precautionary approach. Planning authorities recognise the role of other regimes for pollution control, but see the value of policies in development plans as enabling them to take that precautionary approach.

Annex C

Development Control

C1.1 DEVELOPMENT CONTROL

The basic requirement of planning is that development may not be undertaken without permission from the planning authority. In making decisions on applications for planning permission, the local planning authority must consider the criteria adopted by the local planning authority, including the statutory development plan, and any other material considerations. Those material considerations may include statements of national or regional guidance from central government, and any representations made by other interested parties together with material considerations unique to the site. Development control decisions must accord with the development plan unless material considerations indicate otherwise (PPG1).

Before a planning authority reaches a decision on an application the legislation requires that the application should be placed on a public register and be advertised locally. Any representations made by the public or other organisations should be considered. Certain organisations should also be consulted. In respect of the pollution control agencies:

- the NRA should be consulted on developments involving *inter alia* the retention, treatment or disposal of sewage, trade waste, slurry or sludge;

- in cases where an Environmental Statement has been submitted, HMIP should be consulted on applications for manufacturing industry involving prescribed processes [1].

There is no requirement for Waste Regulation or Local Authority Air Pollution Control authorities to be consulted, but these agencies will have access to the application through the public register and are located within local government. It should be noted that the requirement to consult HMIP only applies to applications subject to EA.

[1] The EA Regulations refer to processes scheduled in regulations under the Health and Safety at Work Act. For new processes these regulations have been replaced by regulations under EPA 1990.

CURRENT GUIDANCE

Guidance is available to planning authorities on the exercise of their development control responsibilities from a number of sources.

C2.1   *MATERIAL PLANNING CONSIDERATIONS*

There are a number of documents which refer to the scope of material planning considerations, and more particularly to pollution control issues in this respect. The thrust of the guidance is that whilst planning should not seek to duplicate controls exercised through other regimes, there may be instances where it is appropriate for planning to intervene to control pollution. Provided a consideration is material in planning terms, it must be taken into account in dealing with a planning application, notwithstanding that other machinery may exist for its regulation (PPG1 Para 30).

Circular 1/85 '**The Use of Conditions in Planning Permissions**' suggests that planning conditions should only be imposed where they are necessary, relevant to planning, relevant to the development to be permitted, enforceable, precise and reasonable in all other respects. Under the criterion of *'relevance to planning'*, a condition would not be appropriate where other controls are also available. However a condition might be needed when the considerations material to the exercise of the two systems of control are substantially different. Therefore, for example, a **planning** condition governing the direction of working on a landfill might be designed to protect the amenities of nearby residents; one within a site licence might relate to the safety aspects of site operations. Planning conditions might also be needed *'since it might be unwise ... to rely on the alternative control being exercised in the manner, or to the degree needed, to secure planning objectives'* (Circular 1/85, para.19).

Further guidance suggests planning intervention is appropriate:

- where the development presents such clear risks to the public that restrictions should be attached or permission refused (MPG 1); and

- where the general interest in the case is wider than the interests of those directly involved in the pollution control regime (Circular 2/85).

Furthermore, it is right for planning authorities to be alert to the possibility of pollution even though there may be a separate regime for its control (Circular 2/85).

It is interesting to note that in discussing the interface between planning and site licensing, Waste Management Paper 26 states that it is *'clearly desirable to establish before planning permission is granted that, with the necessary conditions, a landfill development is likely to qualify for licensing'.* (see Section C2.3)

Further, and more detailed, guidance is given for minerals development.

MPG2 '**Applications, Permissions and Conditions**' states that '*even though matters may be of proper concern to planning, they should not normally be dealt with by means of conditions if they are subject to control under other statutes. A condition which duplicates the effect of other controls will be unnecessary and one whose requirements conflict with those of other controls will be **ultra vires** because it is unreasonable*'. The guidance then goes on to say '*But sometimes good planning considerations may justify imposing conditions dealing with aspects which are at least touched on by other statutes or Common Law*'. It characterises planning conditions as more preventive, whereas alternative legislation may be largely retrospective in effect (MPG2; paras 61 and 62).

MPG7 '**The Reclamation of Mineral Workings**' further distinguishes between planning conditions, which will relate to amenity, access and general landscaping aspects of waste disposal, and waste licence controls designed, for example, to minimize the risk of pollution of water or danger to public health.

C2.2   *PLANNING CONDITIONS AND AGREEMENTS*

Several documents offer examples of planning conditions which are relevant to the interface with pollution control.

- A condition can be imposed requiring a specified action to be taken before development can proceed. This could relate to an aspect of the development not fully described in the planning application which must be submitted for approval, and implemented, before development can begin. Circular 1/85 gives examples of the application of such conditions to drainage and noise control schemes. It is emphasised, however, that such a condition can only be applied if there is a reasonable prospect of the action being taken.

- Circular 1/85 offers model conditions restricting noise at the boundary of a site which, by implication, could be applied to other emissions or releases.

- It also indicates that in very special circumstances it may be appropriate to impose a condition restricting changes in activity which would normally be permitted development (ie because the change is not deemed to be a "material" change). An example is given regarding the storage of hazardous substances. Such conditions should not be used where a more direct condition would achieve the purpose, for example by restricting releases from the site.

- Circular 9/84 also provides that LPA's may restrict the amount, type or location of hazardous substances on site because of the implications for adjoining land use, or to restrict what may happen in the future.

- Waste Management Papers 4 and 26 recognise that planning conditions and agreements are necessary to carry out post-closure controls on landfill sites under the COPA 1974 site licensing regime. WMP 26 gives guidance on arrangements that may be required, and in particular that agreements may be needed to monitor landfill gas.

There is no further specific guidance on the use of agreements, rather than conditions, on pollution control matters. Since 1st January 1992 there is a right of appeal against the terms of Section 106 agreements after a period of 5 years has elapsed from the beginning of the agreement.

A further general matter which is relevant is that Circular 1/85 indicates that a condition cannot be justified on the grounds that the LPA is not the body responsible for the pollution control regime and therefore cannot ensure that it is exercised properly. Nor can it be argued that pollution controls are not permanent and may expire or be renewed. It is acceptable, however, to impose planning conditions where it would be unwise to rely on the alternative control to secure planning objectives.

Current guidance identifies the following circumstances where planning conditions may be appropriate.

- To manage gas on landfill sites, including following closure; and for remedial measures to safeguard filled land for redevelopment (Circular 17/89).

- Control of gas flaring, vehicle routing, equipment on site to minimize noise, means of gas disposal, in the context of the control of oil and gas operations, (Circular 2/85).

- Commencement of development, duration of permission, access, lorry routes, hours of working, where filling of mineral sites is involved (MPG 2).

- Control of dust, smoke and fumes from processing operations associated with mineral extraction (Circular MPG2).

- Control and limitation of noise, smells and dirt from any form of development (para 6.18, PPG 12).

- Height of tip, shape of tip, establishment of grass, shrubs and trees on tipped mineral waste sites (MPG 2).

- Retention of filtering strata in tipped waste to avoid pollution of underground supplies; type of filling material where seepage possible, (MPG 2).

- Protection and conservation of soil resources in reclamation of mineral workings (MPG 7).

- Requirement for detailed site investigations before commencement of development, in case of actual or suspected contaminated land (Circular 21/87 and PPG 14).

In a number of cases it is suggested that problems not solvable by condition can be the subject of Section 106 planning agreements. This applies particularly to gas monitoring at landfills.

The overall test for conditions is given in Circular 1/85. It states that in considering whether a particular condition is necessary, local authorities should ask themselves whether planning permission would have been refused if that condition were not to be imposed. If not, then the condition needs special justification (Circular 1/85; para 12).

C2.3   *DEVELOPMENT CONTROL AND WASTE*

Together, Circulars 21/87 and 17/89 and Waste Management Paper 4 'The Licensing of Waste Facilities' make a number of important points.

- Planning approvals and conditions run with the land; the licence is granted to an operator.

- Planning permission is a pre-requisite to the issue of a site licence for waste disposal. (This is repeated in Part II of the Environmental Protection Act).

  WMP4 states ....'*In making planning permission a pre-requisite ... the intention is to ensure that consideration has been given to the impact on land use of the operation of waste facilities. These considerations include matters such as access, effect on the environmental and visual amenity of the locality and surrounding land uses, the likely nature and duration of the development, hours of operation and relation to policies and proposals in development plans*' (WMP4, para. 3.7).

  The draft PPG on **Noise** discusses the relationship between planning and licensing conditions in respect of noise from landfill sites. It implies that one form of control may act as a **substitute** for the other. It suggests that licence conditions under the Environmental Protection Act 1990 can relate to noise control '*in the interests of protecting local amenity*'. This provision may be used where the site is already operating under an Established Use Certificate or a planning permission not subject to a noise condition. Appropriate planning or licence conditions are considered to relate to hours of working, the number or capacity of vehicles using the site and their points of access, and the provision of screening.

- At present only planning conditions can allow for post closure controls following the termination of a licence (WMP4; paras 3.7 - 3.9). Section 36 of the Environmental Protection Act 1990, when introduced, will empower Waste Regulation Authorities to impose conditions requiring pollution control measures at licensed waste disposal sites to continue as long as may be necessary to make such sites safe. MPG7 nevertheless still sees a role for planning conditions stating that , '*irrespective of these changes, it will remain appropriate for the planning permission to provide for land use aspects of the reclamation of landfilled mineral sites, including details of final levels and contours, the thickness of final covering, the re-spreading of soil layers and subsequent aftercare'* (MPG7; para 31).

- In general terms planning considerations relate to wider matters, such as access and effect on the environmental and visual amenity of the locality; a site licence focuses on the day-to-day control of operations on the site.

- On the relationship between planning and licensing for waste disposal, Waste Management Paper 26 **'Landfilling Waste'**, summarises the situation as follows:

'While planning and licensing may rightly be seen as separate stages through which any proposed landfill development must pass, the close interactions between them must be borne in mind ... Planning permission must be obtained before a waste disposal licence can be issued. On the other hand, it is clearly desirable to establish before planning permission is given that, with necessary conditions, a landfill development is likely to qualify for licensing. Many of the considerations involved will be common to both planning and licensing decisions, and indeed, increasingly, the two stages proceed more or less in parallel' (para 2.3).

Therefore, advice currently stresses that the planning and licensing stages should be complementary, although the planning stage must be completed before a Licence can be granted.

C2.4   *CONSULTATIONS ON DEVELOPMENT CONTROL*

Article 18 of the General Development Order 1988 lists the following circumstances for **statutory** consultation in connection with planning applications:

- Development involving the manufacture processing or keeping of hazardous substances in notifiable quantities (Health and Safety Executive).

- Use of land for depositing refuse or waste (NRA).

- Deposit of sewage, trade waste, slurry or sludge (NRA).

- Developments within 250 metres of land used in the last 30 years for depositing of refuse or waste (Waste Disposal Authority).

It is interesting to note the guidance given on consultation with HSE on planning and major hazards (Circular 9/84). This states that HSE will advise the LPA on the potential hazards associated with development, so that the authority can make a properly informed decision on its planning merits. It recognises that LPAs do not have the necessary expertise and that they need to look to HSE for this advice. The circular then gives advice on the information HSE will need from the LPA to reach a judgement, and on the nature of the response the LPA can expect from HSE. It notes that HSE will be prepared to advise the LPA on the suitability of conditions.

C2.5   *ENVIRONMENTAL ASSESSMENT*

The circumstances in which an environmental assessment will need to be carried out in conjunction with an application for development are outlined in Circular 15/88. Apart from a relatively short list of major projects where assessment is mandatory (schedule 1), the guidance gives most attention to other circumstances in which an assessment may be required (schedule 2).

Projects in schedule 2 will require an assessment if they are likely to give rise to **significant** environmental effects. These may include projects with unusually complex and potentially adverse effects where expert and detailed analysis is desirable. Industrial projects involving emissions which are potentially hazardous to man, or involve the discharge of effluent into the headwaters of rivers, or which otherwise have significant effects far removed from the site are mentioned (Circular 15/88; paras 20 and 28).

For manufacturing plant, indicative criteria suggest that EA may be required where a new plant is 20-30 ha in extent, or is a 'scheduled process' for the purpose of air pollution control, or one involving discharges to water requiring consent of the water authority (now NRA), or when it would give rise to the presence of environmentally significant quantities of potentially hazardous or polluting substances. In the case of landfill, sites with a capacity of more than 75,000 tonnes a year are regarded as possible candidates for EA (Circular 15/88; paras 11 and 23 of Appendix A and EA: A Guide to the Procedures).

In order to make a judgement on the need for an EA under schedule 2 local authorities are encouraged to consult HMIP, HSE and the NRA (Circular 15/88; Appendix A, para 11). Applicants may seek information to assist in the preparation of an Environmental Statement from statutory EA consultees, such as HMIP and NRA. The latter are obliged to provide information which is already in their position and is non-confidential.

Where an EA is carried out for processes prescribed under EPA 1990 (Part I, Part A), the planning authority is required to consult HMIP as well as the normal statutory consultees defined by the GDO.

In this and the following two sections we review the evidence from our research on current practice at the planning-pollution interface in development control. This section deals with material considerations and the use of conditions and agreements. *Section C4* reviews practice regarding consultations with pollution control agencies and *Section C5* deals with a number of other issues relating to pollution and development control. *Section C6* describes a number of planning appeal cases in which pollution and related issues have featured.

C3.1   INTRODUCTION

Our research indicates that there are a number of reasons why local planning authorities either refuse, or attach conditions to planning permission, that relate to the polluting potential of development. These are considered in the sections that follow and are illustrated by reference to case studies.

Our examination of material considerations is organised under seven headings:

- air pollution;
- surface and groundwater protection;
- post-closure pollution from landfill;
- perceptions of pollution risk;
- competence of the operator and complexity of conditions;
- confidence in other regimes;
- need and alternatives.

The evidence is drawn from the planning appeal cases described in *Section C6* and from information provided during interviews with planning authorities. It must be emphasised that all the cases referred to here were conducted prior to implementation of EPA 1990. HMIP was then required to ensure implementation of Best Practicable Means (BPM), a standard widely accepted as being less rigorous than BATNEEC and BPEO, and one that applied only to air emissions.

C3.2   POLLUTION EFFECTS

A number of cases illustrate the role of concern about the effects of pollution as a material planning consideration.

- Glanford District Council objected to permission for a waste treatment centre in a neighbouring district on the grounds that the technology was not proven and the residual risk of air pollution was too great. The main concern was about impact on agricultural interests in the area.

- Delyn District Council refused outline permission for an insulation production plant on the grounds of close proximity to residential property and associated risks of air pollution.

- The Inspector supported refusal of permission for a new chimney to extract paint fumes from a plant in Dudley, on the grounds that the type and size of chimney and the accompanying filters "might go someway to providing a technical solution, but it by no means follows that such a solution is acceptable in planning terms".

- In Gateshead permission for a clinical waste incinerator was refused on grounds that:

  - pollution control processes were unproven;

  - BATNEEC does not necessarily mean zero pollution;

  - there was concern about research indicating a link between incinerators and leukaemia clusters;

  - that if the incinerator operated below capacity or intermittently the plant might perform adversely.

- In Northumberland permission for an animal carcase incinerator that was already operating was refused on the grounds that the equipment was below standard and the site was too close to homes, National Trust property and footpaths, and that adverse weather conditions could trap fumes in the valley.

Cases also illustrate the relevance of existing pollution as a material consideration in applications for potentially sensitive development.

- In an appeal against refusal of permission for residential development, the main issue was whether the effect on the amenity of future residents of odours from a nearby chemical works would justify the refusal. The refusal had been based on the advice of HMIP.

C3.3   SURFACE AND GROUNDWATER PROTECTION

An appeal against a County Council for refusal of planning permission for reclamation of a derelict sandpit by import of waste materials indicates that safeguarding of water resources may be a planning consideration even though there is a separate regime for control. A licensed borehole was located 150m from the site and, although closed, it required protection from the deposit of oils or hydrocarbons. The inspector recognised the importance of the consideration but decided that 'it could be adequately dealt with by the *imposition of appropriate planning conditions and control by the waste regulatory authority'.*

There was an appeal against Stafford Borough Council for refusal of planning permission for a residential development on the grounds that the proposed method of sewage disposal, via septic tanks, represented a potential risk to public health, amenity and a nearby watercourse. Despite the lack of concern expressed by the NRA, the inspector agreed with the Council that the proximity of the septic tank to the proposed development, and the level of the water table, which was believed to be too high to permit the septic tank to operate correctly, carried sufficient risk of pollution and impact on amenity to dismiss the appeal.

The opportunity of siting or modifying developments through the planning system in order to prevent or reduce the possibility of water pollution appears to represent a useful complement to the statutory controls exercised by the NRA via discharge consents. The value of these controls is recognised by authorities such as Ellesmere Port and Neston Borough Council which has standard conditions for oil interceptors and other positive pollution control measures.

C3.4   POST-CLOSURE POLLUTION FROM LANDFILL

Landfill site restoration has long been accepted as a proper subject for planning conditions. Licence conditions may stipulate the method and material to be used in restoration, however, this has also been a condition of planning permission. The motivation for planning conditions in this area has been the need for controls that go with the land as opposed to the operator, who is constrained by site licence conditions. Current arrangements, where the planning authority and the waste regulatory authority are part of the same organisation help to ensure that the conditions of the licence and the planning permission are compatible.

Many cases concern the risks of pollution from landfill sites affecting neighbouring development. A case in Holderness refers to an appeal against an enforcement notice to stop the use of an area of land adjacent to a tip site as a market. The Inspector's report acknowledged paragraph 19 of Circular 17/89 which recognises that the possibilities of difficulties from gas migrating from nearby land can be a material planning consideration in respect of development schemes. The Inspector determined that planning approval would be premature until the likely behaviour of gas had been determined. The Council suggested a form of *"negative condition"* on planning permission, requiring the submission of a detailed scheme for on-going monitoring and gas venting, to the Council. The Inspector doubted the enforceability of such a condition and accepted that other legislation exists in this sphere.

Clearly, it is generally accepted that the migration of gas from a landfill site is a material planning consideration, the potential risks associated with which need to be determined prior to the grant of planning permission for adjacent residential development. It is also acknowledged, however, that conditions requiring monitoring of gas are inappropriate, largely because their enforceability is questionable.

In another case in Stockport the inspector ruled that design details of gas protective measures relating to building construction and site boundaries could be the subject of an appropriate planning condition for a neighbourhood development. Such a condition would appear to be practicable and enforceable.

Another case involved the refusal of a London Borough to grant outline planning permission for a residential development on a site affected by landfill gas. The Borough had objected to a condition suggested by the developer for monitoring the landfill gas after the development, doubting whether it was either lawful or enforceable.

Restoration and aftercare is an area which has seen the use of Section 106 planning agreements to control the actions of operators. The attraction for LPAs of such agreements, which are entered into voluntarily by the developer, lies in their enforceability by the power of injunction, which is not available under a site licence. Consequently, LPAs may continue to regard such agreements as a means of control preferable to the new site licence regime.

C3.5   *PERCEPTION OF POLLUTION RISKS*

The impetus behind controls attempted by local planning authorities is often found to be one of perception of the risk of harm or blight associated with the presence of a potentially polluting installation. It is the local planning authority's purview to consider the potential for an installation to restrict the likelihood of the authority achieving its land use targets by making adjacent areas unattractive to potential developers. They, therefore, consider **perceptions** of pollution as relevant, in contrast to the requirement of the regulatory bodies to consider only the potential for *actual* pollution.

Public perception issues have been of most concern in proposed incinerator developments. Cory Environmental Ltd are currently proposing an incinerator in the London Borough of Bexley which, it is claimed, will be operated *'to the highest pollution control standards and is proposing to fit the most sophisticated emissions reduction equipment available'*. The Council, however, is concerned that the proposal *'would be likely to undermine the investment potential of land zoned for industrial and warehousing use which otherwise could be expected to sustain attractive light industrial development over the next five to seven years'*. The proposal falls within the purview of the Department of Energy and Bexley have lodged an objection. The outcome is yet to be determined.

A similar argument was made by Gateshead MBC in refusing permission for a clinical waste incinerator at Wardley.

An appeal by Cleanaway Ltd against Durham County Council for refusal of planning permission for a chemical waste transfer station also illustrates the influence of public perception in planning issues. The Inspector ruled that with appropriate site licence conditions, no unacceptable risks should arise, but noted that *'I am only too aware of the fears and worries of people who live and work in the area. For this reason any planning permission which is to be given must in my view contain conditions which would ensure reasonable control and safety, even though the subject of such conditions may more usually be in a separate site licence'*. He went on to add that *'Such a site licence applies to a particular operator, and can only be refused for limited reasons. The planning permission applies to the land and suitable conditions can be enforced no matter who the site operator happens to be at any point in time'*. The appeal was granted with conditions regarding the need for suitable surface water disposal arrangements.

An appeal against refusal of permission for a concrete batching plant in Islington was refused on various grounds. Amongst them was the concern of the local community. In this case there were no objective health standards for the pollutant being limited (dust) and the Inspector recognised that in these circumstances the anxiety of local people could not be allayed, and that this should be taken into account.

The influence of public perception is further illustrated by the refusal of Delyn Borough Council to grant permission for a low-level radiation uranium processing plant on the grounds of perceived risk to the local community. This was despite an independent technical report produced for the council which suggested there would be no risk to public health or safety. No appeal was lodged.

C3.6   *THE COMPETENCE OF THE OPERATOR AND COMPLEXITY OF CONDITIONS*

The competence of the operator, in particular with regard to landfilling operations, has been a consideration in a number of cases. In one case several previous breaches of planning conditions or site licence conditions, by the operator, were advanced by a County Council as one reason for not permitting a relaxation on the types of wastes landfilled. The Inspector noted that the operating company had displayed a willingness to act in accordance with their obligations to both local residents and the environment, but also noted that *'with some 150 conditions attached to the permission and site licence 'face workers' find it difficult to comprehend all the various intricacies of waste disposal operations'*. It was the inspector's view that site operatives would be likely to *'short-circuit requirements'* and that *'a grant of permission could lead to undue pressure on the waste disposal authority to accept less than desirable standards.'*

In concluding remarks the inspector expressed confidence *'that the combination of planning conditions and site licence could theoretically establish a safe regime for engineering design, adequate monitoring and the safe processing and disposal of most landfill gas'*.

Attention was also drawn, however, to the practicalities of satisfactory landfilling operations with the comment that the attitude of consultees *'reflects a great reliance on the success of planning and site licence controls without necessarily receiving any guarantees of how or even if these are achievable'*. The need for 150 conditions to ensure satisfactory site operation called into question the advisability of the original grant of planning permission, particularly with regard to enforcement of conditions.

This case illustrates the concern of Inspectors about the ability of an operator to comply with the complexity of conditions that would be required to properly control pollution.

This issue was raised as a consideration in the case of the concrete batching plant in Islington, where the likelihood that the operator could not comply with all the conditions was a factor in dealing with the issue of public confidence in the plant.

C3.7   CONFIDENCE IN OTHER REGIMES

The perception that regulatory bodies may not provide complete controls on pollution has been a frequent motivation for local planning authorities to include pollution control conditions in planning permission. Existing guidance suggests that such conditions should not be included if they are more appropriate under other forms of legislation (Circular 1/85). Consequently the inclusion of such controls has frequently provoked appeals by developers. The concern of local authorities often stems from the previous record of the regulatory bodies which does not give them sufficient confidence to relinquish controls on certain types of development. A contributing factor is the apparent lack of local accountability of the regulatory bodies. Moreover the possibility that the statutory requirement upon HMIP to *'render harmless'* any discharges is actually to *'render as harmless as possible'*, acknowledges that even with appropriate controls there is potential for residual harm.

The Monkton Coke Works in South Tyneside is an on-going dispute in which the Secretary of State has declared that *'it would be unduly onerous and unreasonable to impose, by way of the planning system, a more stringent obligation than is considered necessary by HMIP'*.

Controls on the Land

In a case concerning an application for planning permission for an existing incinerator in Nottinghamshire. The Secretary of State concurred with the Inspector that *"the incineration of chemical waste must be subject to stringent planning controls to overcome the environmental objections"*. The Inspector noted that the courts had found it to be a lawful use of the land. His stated objective was to attempt to achieve a reasonable balance which would *"enable the plant to operate while guaranteeing the improved amenity of the adjacent area"*. He went on to state that...

'It has been argued that the waste licence conditions would ensure adequate plant conditions, but this I cannot accept. Licensing conditions, important as they may be, apply to a particular operator, and that operator cannot be refused a licence except on very limited grounds. That is not sufficient to overcome my worries about this operation in this location. Therefore, it is necessary in my opinion to consider perhaps relatively onerous conditions which apply to any future operator and which go with the land'.

Conditions were thus attached to the permission requiring various site clean-up measures, gas scrubbing, a chimney, and stack gas monitoring in accordance with BPM under advice produced by HMIP.

Parallel Controls

The Ferro-Alloys case involved an appeal against a refusal to grant planning permission for the retention of a 300' chimney at a molybdenum smelting plant. It must be emphasised that this case was not conducted under the provisions of EPA 1990 but under the previous regime in which HMIP has much less effective powers.

An objection to one of the reasons for refusal was that it was not the purview of the local planning authority to use planning conditions to achieve objectives achievable under other legislation. The Inspector found that the planning authority were not trying to exercise parallel control because he was satisfied that they were concerned that they could not rely on an improvement notice, served on the operator by HMIP. It was suggested by the Inspector that, regardless of the grounds for that concern, the planning authorities approach was reasonable. HMIP had indicated that the improvement notice might be reviewed if the operator had financial difficulty in complying with it and if the Inspectorate considered there was no danger to public health. The appeals were granted subject to the condition that: *"The emissions of Sulphur Dioxide from the chimney shall not at any time, after Monday 31 August 1991, exceed 113 kg per hour".*

What emerged was that locally accountable planning authorities either perceived an opportunity to derive increased environmental benefit for an area, or wished to provide themselves with some security against either the failure of the regulatory authorities to implement adequate controls or uncertainties brought about by changes in operators. It has been argued that providing local planning authorities do not seek to impose more stringent controls than the regulatory authorities and also providing that such controls they do impose are enforceable, they should be permitted to do so.

The extent to which such an opportunity is taken will depend on the perceived effectiveness of the regulatory bodies and the prevailing support for intervention at a local level. Whilst some local authorities are willing to follow guidance, others believe strongly in the right to determine a balance between economic and environmental priorities at a local level. It is important that, in adopting the latter course the necessary resources to assess the need for controls and monitor their effectiveness are available.

Cheshire County Council granted outline planning permission for an incinerator after the developer's engineering consultants had suggested that the proposal would be acceptable. When built, the incinerator would not work properly for a period of one year, which was treated by HMIP as an exemption 'commissioning' period. The original scheme had two twenty-metre stacks but engineering changes involved higher stacks and required the developer to apply for a subsequent permission. Cheshire County Council used the opportunity to organise a Section 106 agreement, on the basis of their own technical study, governing many factors that HMIP had not covered since the outline permission. The agreement was in response to local councillor and citizen concerns and covered matters such as:

- 120 hour operability test;
- connection of stack;
- size reduction machinery;
- sampling methods;
- height of chimney;
- emergency issues; and
- extension to the storage area.

Cheshire County Council now take the view that any matters they consider to be inadequately covered by HMIP will, by default, be covered by a legal agreement. They are among a number of authorities that now refuse to grant outline planning permission for potentially polluting development.

Under EPA 1990 this situation should not arise as there is no provision for an exemption period during commissioning. An IPC authorisation would be required before the plant could start to operate.

C3.7   *NEED AND ALTERNATIVES*

Evidence is available from appeal cases in which the consideration of 'need' is balanced against the potential for pollution or environmental degradation arising from a development. Need does not refer to commercial benefit for the developer or proponent, but to an opportunity for provision of a greater good or societal benefit. The argument of 'need' is that an area would benefit from the particular development at the proposed location. There is thus a spatial element to it. At this point the availability of alternatives then becomes relevant. A developer will typically advance a case of need, perhaps supported by an argument that no alternatives exist. The planning authority may counter that alternatives do exist and thus the need argument is consequently diminished. The inspector is required to weigh consideration of pollution potential, need and the availability of alternatives in coming to a decision.

This is illustrated by an appeal by Willment Readymix Concrete Ltd against London Borough of Islington for a concrete batching plant. The case of need was that without a development of this type (to replace an existing one at a nearby site which was to be redeveloped) the building industry in the area would be inadequately supplied with concrete. Furthermore, the site was at a railhead, permitting compliance with a policy of bulk transport of aggregates by rail that would not be available at other sites.

The environmental considerations in this case were the likelihood that the batching plant would be an intrusive source of noise; that an increase in HGV traffic would alter the residential character of surrounding streets; and that dust suppression was contingent upon good operating practice. This last could not be guaranteed and would result in concerns by the local community about the health risk associated with dust emissions. In this, the inspector concluded that the need and the lack of available alternatives were insufficient to outweigh the environmental objections to the development.

A further case involving a consideration of need concerned a landfill site. The provision of adequate capacity in the area, and avoidance of environmental and traffic impacts that would otherwise be involved in transport to more distant alternatives were cited as arguments for the development.

In this case again, however, the considerations of need and lack of alternatives did not outweigh the objections associated with the final landform of the development.

C4.1   INTRODUCTION

This section reviews the views expressed and comments received during interviews, on consultations with the pollution control agencies on development control applications.

Issues raised during interviews are discussed under the following headings:

- LPAs and HMIP;
- LPAs and NRA;
- LPAs and WRAs;
- LPAs and LAPCAs.

C4.2   CONSULTATIONS BETWEEN LPAS AND HMIP

HMIP is a statutory consultee for planning applications involving prescribed processes which are supported by an Environmental Statement (ES). Depending on the level of information provided in the ES, HMIP will comment on a range of issues including: the guidance issued for the process (including BAT options, emission limits and BPEO considerations); any relevant Environmental Quality Objectives; the characteristics of the process; the assessment of options and their environmental impact; and local conditions and the potential for cumulative impact with existing sources in the area. In practice, however, the level of information provided in the ES is rarely sufficient to enable HMIP to provide such detailed comments.

The principal concern of LPAs is that they do not always possess the technical expertise to review certain elements of Environmental Statements. They therefore look to HMIP to provide guidance on the technical merits of proposed schemes. LPAs argue that such guidance is needed to provide a greater degree of certainty that the type of development proposed is appropriate within a particular location. Often they find that HMIP cannot provide this guidance, either because there is insufficient information in the ES or because time and resources are insufficient. In such case planning authorities often call upon other advice, for example, from consultants.

Nature of Response from HMIP

LPAs state that in many instances no response is received from HMIP. It has also been suggested that where comments have been provided, they are rarely in a form which allows LPAs to judge whether the technical measures offered by applicants will be sufficient to meet particular objectives.

Unhelpful responses from HMIP are generally felt to be those which:

- set out pollution control objectives without commenting on the compatibility of particular proposals with those objectives;

- advise that HMIP objects (or does not) without explaining the reasons.

One result of this is that LPAs are beginning to send more specific questions to HMIP as part of consultations. They also take the view, however, that if HMIP does not respond in sufficient detail, pollution matters can be controlled by legal agreements.

Clarification of the Purview of HMIP in the Consultation Process

HMIP stresses the need for LPAs to be made more aware of the types of information they can expect from consultations. Recent internal guidance to inspectors (*Environmental Assessments - Planning and IPC*), for example, states that:

> '... Inspectors should indicate to the planning authorities those aspects of the developer's proposal which are of particular relevance to HMIP's interests, and should comment positively on the environmental statement as far as it relates to these aspects ... '.

It is also suggested that LPAs are not always fully aware of the range of issues considered by the Inspectorate. In the same guidance, HMIP states that:

> '... (EA consultations) provide an opportunity to set out HMIP's view of environmental constraints for that area, with any particular aspects that should be avoided ...'.

Timing Of Response From HMIP

LPAs are mindful of the need to determine planning applications supported by an ES within a sixteen week period. A common concern is that HMIP often fails to provide a timely formal response. Furthermore, many LPAs have suggested that the internal structure of HMIP does not lend itself to obtaining informal telephone responses within a shorter period.

In response, some LPAs have begun to enter into discussions with HMIP about developing a protocol for handling consultations. However, the need for more systematic guidelines on consultation procedures is widely recognised.

C4.3 CONSULTATION BETWEEN LPA AND NRA

The statutory requirement for NRA to be consulted specifically includes developments discharging trade effluents. NRA recognises, that many of its pollution control objectives can be reinforced by planning controls. It therefore tends to take a proactive stance in relation to planning applications.

The degree of involvement varies between regions; in some areas NRA monitors the planning register on a regular basis and actively contacts the planning authority on relevant applications, in others, the LPA sends weekly lists of all new applications. All NRA regional offices have appointed Town and Country Planning liaison officers who define procedures for dealing with consultation on planning applications.

The principal concerns of LPAs when consulting NRA, are that the Authority does not always respond within an adequate timescale or in an appropriate form to assist the decision-making process. These issues are dealt with in more detail below.

Form of Response from NRA

Responses received from NRA vary considerably from detailed discussion of the merits of development proposals and requirements for detailed planning conditions, to simple statements of no objection. Responses which are considered unhelpful included:

- responses suggesting environmental objectives that should be sought but offering no technical guidance on the measures needed to achieve them; for example requiring that a drainage system be installed to achieve satisfactory drainage of land, but not describing the type of system required;

- responses offering standard "off-the-shelf" conditions which appear to take no account of the particular circumstances of the development.

NRA is a statutory consultee for many types of development because of its wide ranging interests. It therefore makes quite extensive use of standard reply formats for consultation. It was, however, pointed out to us that replies which were too evidently 'off-the-shelf' could present difficulties for planning officers trying to persuade members of the merits of the NRA's arguments.

NRA has noted that a satisfactory response to consultations is more likely if a set of specific questions is posed. To this end at least one NRA regional office has issued a protocol which sets out the type of information the agency needs from LPAs to provide a complete response.

Timing of Response from NRA

Many LPAs have noted that NRA often fails to provide a timely formal response. Further, although informal (ie telephone) responses may be obtained more easily than with HMIP, there is no guarantee that this will be confirmed by the formal response.

NRA acknowledges a slowness of response in some instances, but suggests that the time taken to respond is largely a function of the range of issues requiring comment and consequently, the numbers of officers involved.

CONSTULTATIONS BETWEEN LPAS AND WASTE REGULATION AUTHORITIES (WRA)

There is no statutory requirement for LPAs to consult WRAs on planning applications for new waste disposal sites, nor is the WRA obliged to consult the LPA on site licensing issues. There is, however, a statutory requirement for LPAs to consult WRAs on development proposals within 250 metres of former and existing landfill sites, as well as sites which have been notified to the LPA for the purposes of this provision.

Planning Applications for New Waste Disposal Sites

In practice, LPAs and WRAs appear to cooperate very closely on planning applications for new waste disposal sites. LPAs argue that because the waste technical, site operation and access arrangements are intimately linked with site licensing, there is a wide interface between the planning and licensing functions. Indeed, in the majority of cases, applicants are required de facto to make planning and site licensing applications at the same time.

It is suggested that consideration of applications concurrently ensures that LPAs and WRAs develop a common position from the outset. Close cooperation enables the two authorities to establish which conditions should be attached to the planning application and which to the site licence.

The principal concern of LPAs is that their ability to cooperate on planning and site licensing issues will be weakened if WRA functions are transferred to a new Environment Agency.

It has also been suggested that there is a need for closer cooperation on the waste implications of planning applications generally. Many WRAs, for example, have commented that it would be useful if they were consulted more systematically on the waste generation potential of development proposals, particularly when the planning and waste regulatory functions do not operate from the same authority.

Planning Applications in the Vicinity of Waste Disposal Sites

A number of concerns have been raised in relation to development proposals in the vicinity of former, existing or future landfill sites. In the case of former landfill sites, concerns relate mainly to the ability of LPAs to evaluate every aspect of potential risk. LPAs tend to place a strong reliance on Environmental Health Departments for technical advice, but are often uncertain of the technical competence of these Departments in certain areas. LPAs argue that there is little guidance for dealing with applications in the vicinity of landfill sites and consequently a lack of consistency between different authorities on pollution control issues. It has also been suggested that authorities are over-protective; many choose to treat the 250 metre consultation zone as a *cordon sanitaire*, for example.

For existing landfill sites, the main concern of LPAs is that there is no statutory route for raising objections to a proposed amendment to a current site licence. Furthermore, the WRA cannot unreasonably refuse such applications if they do not contravene the conditions set out in the planning permission.

The concern is that LPAs cannot be expected to anticipate all possible future amendments to a licence at the time of determining the original planning application. Furthermore, no system is in place to ensure that adequate consideration is subsequently given to planning concerns. These concerns include public perceptions of risk and commercial blight in the surrounding area. Such concerns apply equally to areas which have been allocated for future landfill.

C4.5   *CONSULTATIONS BETWEEN LPA AND LOCAL AUTHORITY AIR POLLUTION CONTROL AUTHORITIES (LAAPC)*

There are no formal procedures for consultation between LPAs and LAAPC Authorities. Public registers provide the only formal route by which LAAPC Authorities can raise objections to a proposal. In practice, however, there is a great deal of cooperation between the two authorities and most LPAs use LAAPC authorities (usually Environment or Environmental Health Departments) as a principal source of advice on pollution control issues. This seems to be particularly the case for developments involving IPC processes which are not subject to EA and are therefore not formally commented on by HMIP.

The main concern of LPAs is that LAAPC Authorities are not in a position to comment on all aspects of pollution control. Further, many LPAs argue that in the absence of further involvement on the part of HMIP, few alternative routes are currently available for obtaining technical advice. It has been suggested that extending the requirement for EA to all prescribed processes, could go a long way to solving these problems.

The Secretary of State has issued 76 guidance notes for LAAPC, following consultation with HMIP, local authorities, industry representatives and environmental groups. These indicate BATNEEC for scheduled processes under Local Authority control. This will reinforce the reportedly useful relationship between HMIP and LAAPC and may contribute to an improvement in the result of consultations between LPAs and LAAPC Authorities.

C5.1　INTRODUCTION

During the course of the study, interviews with the regulatory bodies, local authorities and other interested parties revealed a number of other issues which were of concern. These are considered in turn in the sections that follow.

C5.2　TIMING OF APPLICATIONS

A cause of uncertainty is the timing of applications for planning permission and for authorisation or licensing. Each type of assent is perceived by developers as a separate requirement. The level of information necessary for an application for authorisation or licensing is generally more precise and detailed than that required for planning permission. Consequently more development work is required, with associated time and cost penalties, than is required for planning permission. A developer, therefore, would be very unwilling to invest resources in full process design until the first hurdle of planning permission is cleared. Unfortunately, it is at the stage of determining planning applications that the conflict between the remit of the regulatory bodies and the requirements of the LPAs is most evident.

As pollution, or the risk or perception of it, can be a material planning consideration, the local authority requires a clear indication of the likely potential effects of the development at the time at which it determines the application. As stated previously, however, this information may not be available, being dependent upon details of process design, plant and operating regimes, which have yet to be determined. Two factors, also considered in C4 are relevant: consultation procedures, and the use of EA. As indicated in C4 the advice currently obtained by planning authorities from the regulatory bodies at this stage is far from adequate and recommendations are included in *Section 4* of this report as to how this may be improved. As regards EA, it is apparent that an EA accompanying an application for a potentially polluting installation may be inadequate, and fail to comply with EA Regulations, if it does not accurately reflect the potential impacts on the environment.

These deficiencies indicate a need for further guidance on the scope and detail of EA. At the planning stage the developer should provide a 'worst case' estimate of the likely effects of a development. This will enable the LPA to determine whether or not the proposal will have **an unacceptable impact on the environment.**

The application for IPC authorisation subsequently requires a more detailed and precise estimate of pollution impacts, based on information drawn from a more detailed design specification than that available at the planning stage. It must also take into account many other aspects of operating and management practice (eg staffing, training, etc). At the pollution control stage the regulatory agencies will be concerned to determine that the proposal is designed to release **the minimum possible amount of pollution** to the environment. Consequently, there is the potential for IPC authorisation to stipulate stricter standards than may be deemed necessary at the planning stage. The expectation of HMIP is that this will often be the case.

It is important to indicate the distinction between IPC authorisation and the procedure of waste disposal site licencing. It has been found in practice that many controls on such sites can be exercised either through the planning or the licensing system. Consequently, and in contrast to the IPC authorisation, the two approaches tend to operate more in parallel. This approach is operated as a requirement by Durham County Council who require the WRA, the LPA and the prospective operator to hold joint discussions and proceed in parallel towards planning permission and licensing.

During the course of the study a number of references were made by consultees regarding the inadvisability of granting outline planning permission for potentially polluting developments (see Cheshire County Council, *Section C3.7*). The concern is that an adequate assessment of the potential environmental effects of a development cannot be made from an outline planning application and any such permission potentially places constraints on subsequent requirements of pollution abatement technology. An iterative process involving timely consultation with the LPA and the pollution control authority should be recommended to developers.

A further modification would be a requirement for EA on any development involving a process prescribed for IPC. At present the EA Regulations require EA for particular types of *development* whilst IPC Authorisation is related to types of *process*. A rationalisation of these requirements would ensure that all processes with the potential to cause serious pollution were reported on at the planning stage.

C5.3   *LOCAL ACCOUNTABILITY VS A STRATEGIC APPROACH*

LPAs are ultimately accountable to a local constituency in a way that regulatory authorities are not. As a result they are kept more aware of local concerns and are open to local political influence. Consequently, pressure exists to provide controls on industry at a local level, and results in planning refusals and conditions of the type already described.

A need is perceived for positive planning to accommodate industry and waste sites. Planning authorities are reluctant to adopt this locational approach, however, on the grounds that it would blight areas adjacent to those designated for such use.

Developers are in favour of a more strategic approach to controls on this type of industry. The benefit to them would include a consistency of approach and application of standards. There is also an appreciation of the need for a strategic identification of requirements for certain types of facility (such as chemical waste facilities), allied to regional self sufficiency in provision of waste management capacity.

C5.4   *AGREEMENTS*

Increasing use of Section 106 Agreements between LPAs and developers is being made to control operations at waste disposal sites. Provisions available under the new waste licences should in theory remove the need for such agreements, however, it is recognised that Section 106 Agreements provide the power of injunction and thus may be more easily enforced.

C5.5   *WATER RESOURCES*

As a consultee to planning applications the NRA has the opportunity to influence the control of potentially polluting installations in a way that is not available through their powers to license discharges. The NRA's controls are "*end of pipe*", requiring a standard of discharge to be met in order that statutory water quality objectives (under the Water Resources Act 1991) may be achieved. The NRA may also suggest preventive measures via the planning system which contribute to the safeguarding of water quality.

Evidence suggests that the NRA is adopting a positive approach to identifying planning applications with the potential to affect water resources. The Draft document 'Policy and Practice for the Protection of Groundwater', states in relation to the Town and Country Planning Act 1990:

> '*Many developments may pose a direct or indirect threat to groundwater resources. Where planning permission is required (eg chemical stores, residential development, mineral extraction, industrial development) often the only control is by means of conditions on the permission document, or by refusal of permission.*'

C6.1   DAVID RIBY AGAINST AN ENFORCEMENT NOTICE ISSUE BY HOLDERNESS
BOROUGH COUNCIL CONCERNING THE USE OF LAND AND BUILDINGS AT
WESTFIELD FARM, SIGGLESHTHORNE (MAY 1991)

An appeal was made against an enforcement notice to stop using an area of
land as a market. Immediately east of the market is a large tip site in a
former sand and gravel quarry. Access was the main issue. The second
issue involved ongoing landfill gas production. It was the view of the
County Council as WDA that a full appraisal of actual and potential
contamination from landfill gas was a prerequisite for any development
proposal at the site. Circular 17/89 'Landfill Sites: Development Control'
paragraph 19 recognises that the possibility of difficulties from gas migrating
from nearby land can be a material planning consideration in respect of
development schemes. The argument centred around what were *'reliable
arrangements to overcome the danger of migrating gas: initial appraisal and long-
term monitoring'*. It was determined that it would be premature to grant
permission until the likely behaviour of gas was determined. The Inspector
was *'invited to consider a form of negative condition of planning permission
requiring the submission of a detailed scheme* [of on-going monitoring and gas
venting] *to the council'*.

The Inspector doubted the enforceability of a negative condition for
monitoring and control of landfill gas. He accepted that *'other legislation
exists in this sphere, and that it was necessary to be satisfied that control measures
could be reasonably applied to ensure safety before planning permission is granted
on a site potentially at risk'*. It was concluded, therefore, that it was premature
to grant planning permission to the development.

C6.2   BARRATT MANCHESTER LTD AGAINST HYNDBURN BOROUGH COUNCIL FOR THE
FAILURE TO DETERMINE AN APPLICATION FOR A RESIDENTIAL DEVELOPMENT
(FEBRUARY 1991)

The issues in this case were the proximity of the site to works notifiable
under Control of Industrial Major Accident Hazards (CIMAH) Regulations,
together with the potential effects of any landfill gas which might be
generated by a former landfill. The site is part of a larger area where outline
planning permission was granted in 1973 for 190 dwellings. The Borough
Planning Officers report to the Council indicated that, subject to the landfill
gas monitoring being satisfactory, the proposals should be conditionally
approved. The proposals were found to be *'consistent with operative
development plan policies'*. The Health and Safety Executive (HSE) indicated
that there were *'no strong grounds for refusal'* as the site was over 400m
distant. The local council expressed reservations and acknowledged
residents' concerns.

The Inspector took HSE's word as the *best available advice* and found that proximity to the CIMAH installation was insufficient grounds for refusal.

The landfill gas assessor assisting the Inspector found that: *'The local planning authority in the face of the evidence it had before it could not reasonably have come to the conclusion that the development could be approved until the landfill gas issues were resolved'* but also concluded that it was *'unlikely to be a major problem'*. The Inspector decided that with adequate gas protection measures included in the design of the buildings the development could be acceptable.

The Council suggested a condition concerning prevention of landfill gas ingress into structures. The appellants were concerned about this and suggested incorporation of a previously accepted design by the WDA for plots within 250m of the landfill site. The assessor pointed out that gas might also arrive from other sources eg. mines, and that protection measures on structures, irrespective of location, were appropriate. Therefore, the Inspector approved the development with the following condition (amongst others):

'Appropriate ground treatment and/or building construction measures shall be incorporated into the development of the site for the purpose of preventing gas ingress into all structures. None of the development hereby approved shall be commenced until details of such measures have been submitted to and approved in writing by the Local Planning Authority.'

C6.3   *MR AND MRS ERRINGTON AGAINST NORTHUMBERLAND COUNTY COUNCIL FOR FAILURE TO DETERMINE AN APPLICATION FOR INCINERATOR AND BUILDINGS (JANUARY 1990)*

The development had already commenced. The issue was whether, "*in the light of local policies to protect the character of the countryside and enhance the tourist industry, the incinerator would be likely to cause unacceptable smells*". The incinerator is used as part of a pet cremation service.

The surrounding countryside is an Area of Great Landscape Value as defined in the 1956 Approved County Development Plan: New structure plan policies require that development *'has regard to the inherent qualities of the environment, and conserves its character and quality'*. It is the intention to prevent, as far as practicable, the pollution of air and water. National policy on this subject is that small enterprises are acceptable in rural areas as long as they don't intrude in the countryside or generate smell.

Evidence given at the enquiry was not conclusive on the question of whether or not smells were generated. But the equipment of the incinerator was deemed to be below standard for the task (it did not comply with guidance in Waste Management Paper 4 or with the relevant British Standard (BS3136).

The Inspector drew attention to the proximity of dwellings, a National Trust property visited by 140,000 people/year, footpaths close to the site and the fact that under some weather conditions fumes may be held in the valley. He cited approved strategic policies to protect designated countryside and enhance tourism and considered *'that the incinerator is not appropriate in this location'*.

The County Council had stated that *'only the difficulty in applying and enforcing conditions on the use held back the grant of planning permission'*.

Therefore, despite no nuisance having been proved, the fact that the potential for it existed and that the development ran contrary to approved strategic policies was enough to dismiss the appeal.

C6.4   *V N TAPP ESQ AND THE FORD AND SLATER GROUP AGAINST THE REFUSAL OF NORTH KESTEVEN DISTRICT COUNCIL TO GRANT A PLANNING PERMISSION FOR RESIDENTIAL DEVELOPMENT (JUNE 1989)*

The proposal was for residential development in the vicinity of existing industrial uses. The structure and other plans relevant to the area were very dated but the proposal was found by the Inspector to *'constitute a departure from longstanding land use designation'* (ie. industrial).

The Inspector considered that *'if the appeal sites were released then it would place residential premises directly alongside active industrial uses .... would inhibit freedom of use in the industrial units'*. This could arise from complaints over smell, noise, unsocial working hours and could prejudice future industrial redevelopment. The Inspector also foresaw the necessity of *'mounding to attenuate noise'* and therefore sterilisation of a 70m wide strip which would *'not make best use of available land and would run contrary to paragraph 12, Annex A in Circular 15/84'*. He considered that if proposals were to proceed then *'I am convinced their relationship would be volatile and lead to an irrevocable and inordinate change in the character and appearance of the locality which would constitute demonstrable harm of the kind referred to in Circular 14/85.*

C6.5   *CORY SAND AND BALLAST LIMITED AGAINST THE REFUSAL BY LONDON BOROUGH OF BEXLEY TO GRANT PLANNING PERMISSION FOR A RESIDENTIAL DEVELOPMENT (JULY 1990)*

The Inspector considered that the issue was *'whether the available information gives sufficient assurance that the inhabitants of the development would be safe from the hazards of landfill gas for the foreseeable future'*. Attention was drawn to ICRCL 17/78 which states that *'sites known to be producing landfill gas are best avoided for all forms of hard development'*. The Inspector found that insufficient site investigations had occurred. Also that it could not be guaranteed, with housing as a use, that an adequate site management regime would be continued whilst the site was still gassing.

Bexley objected to a condition suggested by the developer for monitoring the landfill gas *'after the development'* doubting whether it was either *'lawful or enforceable'*: and because it seemed to imply a Section 52 Agreement which

H

they would not wish to sign because of the unacceptable liability of an event such as an explosion.

The Secretary of State agreed with the Inspector's dismissal of the appeal.

C6.6   *MR AND MRS DOMMETT AGAINST EAST DEVON DISTRICT COUNCIL FOR REFUSAL OF PLANNING PERMISSION FOR FIVE SMALL CRAFT UNITS IN A RESIDENTIAL AREA (JUNE 1989)*

The appeal was dismissed because properties were so close to the site that *'relatively small amounts of smell, fumes, dust and vibration generated by activities associated with any one of the five units would be noticed by residents.*

C6.7   *YEMM HOLDINGS LIMITED AGAINST TAFF-ELY BOROUGH COUNCIL FOR REFUSAL OF PLANNING PERMISSION FOR A RESIDENTIAL DEVELOPMENT (OCTOBER 1990)*

The issue was determined by the Inspector to be *'whether the possible effects on the amenities of future occupiers of dwellings on the site by reason of odours emanating from the nearby chemical works would justify the refusal of the proposed development'*. In the local plan, the site has no notation. It used to be industrial use but that ceased in 1987. The area around the site is mainly residential and community use.

The reasons for refusal by the Borough Council were on the recommendation of HMIP. The Principal Inspector stated that *'while BPM was employed in the operation of the works, numerous complaints have been received about the emission of a fishy-type odour'*. The Council has said that use of the amine chemical does not affect the health of people. No data is available regarding the frequency or location of complaints, although the Council claimed that most of the immediate area has suffered.

In the Inspector's opinion the principle of residential use on the site was acceptable (due to similar surrounding uses) and it does not lie within a location where the prevailing wind would bring odours. He acknowledged that the evidence suggests that future occupiers would, as with other residents, have their amenities affected at some times, but concludes: *'Nevertheless, I consider that no compelling evidence has been provided to demonstrate why planning permission on this particular site should not be forthcoming'*.

Consequently outline planning permission was granted with no relevant conditions.

This case involved competing demands for the use of a site for industry or housing. Two main issues required determination. The first was *'the impact of employment and housing policies, and the balance between their competing requirements'* and the second was noise. After considering the site surroundings and likely constraints the inspector determined that industrial usage would probably be constrained, and further, that the need to retain the land for industrial purposes was not overwhelming. A generally *'insatiable demand for housing'* and a requirement in RPG3 for 9,000 additional dwellings by 2001 were noted by the inspector who accepted that housing would be an appropriate use. It would *'relate well to the conservation area and the environmental corridor and would give opportunity for enhancement.'* In conclusion the inspector did *'not find objection to either form of development on this site'* but continued that neither *'has such an urgent need as to preclude the other'*.

It is apparent, therefore, that suitability of the site for both types of development was established but a pressing *need* for either one of the two was not. Consequently, when site investigations by the inspector and his noise assessor determined that noise from an adjacent factory would be unacceptable , he concluded, *'..... there would be a substantial potential for complaints. This by itself may not be a direct planning issue but in my judgement it would be wrong, having regard to health and quality of the living environment, to put houses and their occupiers into this position'*.

C6.9

J AND W LIMITED AGAINST HAMPSHIRE COUNTY COUNCIL FOR FAILURE TO DETERMINE AN APPLICATION FOR RESTORATION OF AGRICULTURAL LAND USING WASTE MATERIALS (MAY 1991)

The Inspector determined that the issues in this case were:

- acceptability of the proposed development, having regard to planning policies related to waste disposal and the environment

- effect on amenity of local residents by visual intrusion, noise, dust, smells and traffic generated;

- other traffic issues.

The site involved approximately 15 ha of Grade 4 agricultural land. The proposal was to tip about 630,000m³ of inert wastes. It was found that the development was in concurrence with general policies on waste disposal:

'The site clearly lies in an area wherein both the local (the Structure Plan and Winchester Southern Parishes Local Plan) and national policies seek to normally restrain development. Waste disposal by land raising, however, is a temporary use of land which would be inappropriate in a built-up area. It seems to me that

providing there would be no long-term harm to the local environment, the proposal may be allowed as an exception to the normal restriction to development in the countryside.'

It was also found, however, that the landform as proposed would appear manmade and would detract from the appearance of the locality, contrary to the aims of Structure Plan Policy E3 and that it would conflict with the aims of the relevant WMP policies insofar that land raising proposals should not give rise to unacceptable environmental impact. The issue was thus dismissed.

The question of need was also considered by the inspector. In reference to the Hampshire Waste Management Plan, it was noted *"that there is a shortfall in capacity to deal with waste arising to 2001"* and further that *"the County Surveyor (Waste Disposal) raised no objection to the proposal because of the shortfall in capacity"*.

The inspector then considered the weight to be given to various policies with a bearing on the case. Requirements for *'efficient and environmentally acceptable means of waste disposal'* and that *'the County ensures that sufficient facilities are provided to meet demands for wastes disposal'* were noted. Furthermore, a policy which sought to normally restrict land raising but did not preclude its consideration where no reasonable practicable alternatives were available, was mentioned.

The inspector concluded that *'Given the shortfall in capacity and the lack of guidance on the extent to which land raising should form part of waste disposal policy, I consider that the proposed development would not in principle materially conflict with these relevant planning policies.'*

The inspector went on to note, however, other relevant policies which *'seek to ensure that the environmental impact of a specific proposal would not be unacceptable.'* At this point the need to consider *the site specific terms of the proposal* is highlighted. A discussion followed regarding the potential visual impact of the development. This was finally determined to be the key factor, overriding the established *need* for the development.

The Inspector stated that tipping would be controlled by a Waste Disposal Licence which would *'impose considerable controls on the material which may be deposited and ensure it would be limited to inert material free of putrescible waste which could give rise to smells, pollution and attract vermin. Measures to suppress dust and fumes could be incorporated into the site activities in accordance with planning conditions'*. The Inspector was, therefore satisfied that amenity would not be harmed and that he could not refuse on the second issue.

It was concluded that: *'.... the landform would be out of keeping and detract from the appearance of the local landscape contrary to the aims of policies which seek to protect the environment. The protection of the countryside from unacceptable development is an interest of acknowledged importance. The proposal would harm that interest and amounts to demonstrable harm sufficient, in my view, to turn the proposal away, even given the need for the development.'*

C6.10   NSM WASTE CONTROL LIMITED AGAINST THE REFUSAL BY LEICESTERSHIRE CITY COUNCIL OF PLANNING PERMISSION FOR THE RECLAMATION OF A SANDPIT THROUGH CONTINUATION OF IMPORTATION OF WASTE MATERIALS (APRIL 1991)

The Inspector noted that an issue *'to which the NRA and others have drawn my attention is that there is a groundwater borehole about 150m from the site. Although closed, this is still licensed and hence needs to be protected, especially from the deposit of oils or hydrocarbons. In my view, although this is an important consideration it could be adequately dealt with by the imposition of appropriate planning conditions and control by the waste regulatory authority. I also consider that the protection of the brook from pollution would be primarily a matter for the latter authority.'* As a consequence the case did not turn on this issue and was determined on the basis of three others, being dismissed on grounds of effect on agricultural land.

C6.11   GLADMAN HOMES AGAINST THE REFUSAL BY STAFFORD BOROUGH COUNCIL TO APPROVE DETAILS RESERVED BY OUTLINE PLANNING PERMISSION FOR A RESIDENTIAL DEVELOPMENT (SEPTEMBER 1991)

The main issue was deemed to be the effect the proposed method of sewage disposal (septic tank) would have on the nearby watercourse, public health in general, and the amenities of occupiers of the proposed houses.

The Foul sewer lay 100m north of the site. The Water Authority (WA) had indicated that additional flows to the small treatment plant via the sewer would be likely to cause it to fail to comply with the *strict* discharge consent under which it operated. Improvement works by the WA were due to be completed in December 1992.

Outline planning permission indicated that disposal would be via mains sewer but no objection was received from the WA at that time. Plots one to six were developed with septic tanks. Septic tank disposal was now proposed for plot seven.

The Council stated that the proximity of the proposed dwelling to its septic tank and other septic tanks would likely result in harmful effects to the living conditions of prospective residents, especially from smells. The Council also believed that there was a potential risk of pollution to the watercourse, despite the Council having recently granted permission for similar arrangements to the west. The Water Authority and NRA have raised no objections in this case. Despite this, the Inspector stated that because of the proximity of the septic tank to the house (less than 15m) and the level of the watertable which he believes to be too high to permit the septic tank to operate correctly, he considered that risk of pollution and impact on amenity is sufficient to dismiss the appeal, ie he concurred with the council (despite their previous behaviour in similar situations) and disagreed with NRA.

C6.12   *SAILPORT PLC AGAINST THE REFUSAL BY PORTSMOUTH CITY COUNCIL FOR PLANNING PERMISSION TO EXTEND EXISTING MARINA (JUNE 1991)*

The third issue, after questions of visual intrusion and access, was determined by the Inspector to be whether there would be a *'harmful increase in the levels of untreated sewage in the estuary.'*

Sewage will arise directly from boats and from onshore facilities which discharge direct into the estuary. The Environmental Health Officers report to members, regarding the direct discharge from boats (1990) raised no objections to the proposal. The Inspector believed that in practice self regulation by Marina users would prevail, and so direct discharge would not be a problem.

Regarding sewage disposal from the sewer, the NRA raised no objections. It was undisputed that the extension of the marina would increase discharges to the estuary. The NRA representative indicated that the estuary receives untreated sewage from a number of outfalls and "*does not at present meet the standards required by the authority under National and European Legislation*". He concurred that increases, however small, in an already unacceptable situation were bound to make it worse.

It was noted that this outfall was not the worst offender, that it discharges into deep water of the ebb tide thus aiding dilution. It was stated that considerable efforts were being made by competent authorities to ensure compliance as soon as practicable. In Autumn 1992, the consent is due to be reviewed. The Water Company was stated to have plans to eliminate untreated discharges by mid 1990's. In the meantime, a schedule of recommended development restrictions had been formalised between NRA and the Council, and would apply to future proposals.

The Inspector acknowledged public concern but concluded that in *'the particular circumstances of this case the balance of judgement should lie in favour of permitting the development'*. He was satisfied that this case would not weaken the ability of the NRA to make appropriate representations on future planning applications or the ability of the Council to resist new proposals which would add to problems of Water Quality in the estuary and found further that the "*objections of the Council ..... outweighed by the benefits of the proposal*". These *'benefits'* were mainly local employment opportunities.

The Inspector allowed the appeal, and attached no conditions regarding water pollution.

SUMMERLEAZE LIMITED AGAINST THE ROYAL COUNTY OF BERKSHIRE COUNCIL TO REFUSE PLANNING PERMISSION FOR AN AMENDMENT TO A CONDITION REGARDING A WASTE DISPOSAL SITE (JULY 1991)

The removal of the condition was sought to allow extension of the range of imported wastes to include household and civic amenity wastes. The condition in dispute stated:

'the deposit of waste materials shall proceed progressively behind the extraction operation and only industrial, commercial and inert waste as specified in conditions attached to any waste disposal licence issued in respect of the site under the Control of Pollution Act 1974 or subsequent amendments thereof shall be deposited at the site and inert waste only shall be deposited within the following margins:-

i)   *150m of houses east of Lodge Road*
ii)   *65m of the River Lodden*
iii)   *40m of Emm Brook*
iv)   *30m of the proposed new lakes*
v)   *6m of the proposed new ditches*

unless otherwise authorised by the County Planning Authority'.

The Inspector determined that *'The crux of this appeal revolves round the existing and desired composition of tipped material and the consequences stemming therefrom'.*

It appears, therefore, that the appellants wished to change a planning condition that *requires* compliance with a WD licence and extends the range of site operating conditions.

Regarding the Management Record of the operator; several previous breaches of planning conditions/site licence conditions were advanced by the Council. The Inspector noted, however, that *'with some 150 conditions attached to the permission and site licence 'face workers' find it difficult to comprehend all the various intricacies of waste disposal operations'.* This raises the issue of enforceability of conditions and the possibility that an excessive list of requirements for site operation may be counter-productive.

The Inspector also expressed doubts over borehole evidence and the compatibility of local strata with the needs of a containment site. It was noted that gas and leachate are covered by the licence during operation but that when the site is complete there is no indication of proposals for dealing with ongoing production.

The WDA had stated that they did not intend changing their monitoring procedure but the Inspector writes of *'disquiet which stems from the number of breaches spotted by local residents that planning permission apparently remain undetected by the WDA'*

The Inspector accepted that adequate site operations would be possible in theory. Attention was drawn to the attitude of consultees which *'reflects a great reliance on the success of planning and site licence controls without necessarily receiving any guarantees of how or even if these are achievable'.*

The Inspector stated that it was likely that site operatives would short-circuit requirements and that *'a grant of permission could lead to undue pressure on the WDA to accept less than desirable standards'.*

The reasons for dismissal were stated to be:

- lack of borehole data
- lack of Leachate composition data; and
- the previous management record of the operator.

It was further stated that monitoring the proportion of household waste would be unenforceable.

C6.14   *CORREX METALS LIMITED AGAINST ROCHDALE METROPOLITAN BOROUGH COUNCIL FOR THE REFUSAL OF PLANNING PERMISSION FOR THE CONTINUED USE OF A WASTE TRANSFER STATION (JUNE 1991)*

This appeal was granted, subject to planning conditions limiting noise at the site boundary to a one minute L_{eq} of 60dB(A).

C6.15   *GRIFFIN CAR BODIES LIMITED AGAINST DUDLEY METROPOLITAN BOROUGH COUNCIL FOR TWO ENFORCEMENT NOTICES AND A PLANNING REFUSAL (FEBRUARY 1991)*

This case involved a chimney to extract fumes from a paint shop. The Inspector found that it was *'likely to give rise to unacceptable nuisance to residents by reason of smell and noise - and so far as smell is concerned there is evidence that this in practice occurs from time-to-time'.*

It was further stated that *'A chimney of this type and size, and its accompanying filters might go some way to providing a technical solution to the process being undertaken but it by no means follows that such a solution is acceptable in planning terms, particularly when, as in the present instance, the process itself requires planning permission'.*

C6.16   *WILLMENT READYMIX CONCRETE LIMITED AGAINST LONDON BOROUGH OF ISLINGTON FOR REFUSAL OF PLANNING PERMISSION FOR A RAILHEAD AGGREGATES DEPOT AND CONCRETE BATCHING PLANT (JULY 1991)*

Three issues are of interest in relation to this appeal.

1. Need and Alternatives

The appellant argued that there was a need for the development to be located in the area and there were no other acceptable alternative sites to the one proposed. They argued that the need and the lack of alternatives were sufficient to overcome the objections, which were principally concerned with impacts on residents caused by noise, dust and traffic. The Inspector recognised need and the lack of alternatives as valid considerations in the case saying:

> 'These matters [the harm to residential amenity] *should be balanced against the need for the development ....'*

> 'the situation relating to alternative locations for a plant .... lends ... additional support to the Appellants' case on commercial need.'

In this instance he concluded, however, that the need and the lack of alternatives were insufficient to outweigh the objections.

2. Perceptions of Pollution Risk

Dust was recognised as a potential problem with the application and the appellants had agreed to numerous measures to control dust. The Inspector did note, however, that there was no detailed evidence as to the significance for public health of the level of control achievable. He concluded that:

> 'In the absence of any clear medically based standards for harmful ... concentrations in the atmosphere, the possible risks to health of persons susceptible to respiratory complaints ... should nevertheless be taken into account, and also the anxiety about such risks, which is extensively reflected in representations on the appeal ...'

> 'Where it is not possible to reassure local people objectively about the level of risk ... it seems to me that ... a large number of people would continue on a long term basis to feel ill at ease about the impact on health. As it does not seem possible to allay such fears ... entirely and objectively, this anxiety is real, and should in my opinion be recognised in the decision on the appeal'.

3. Complexity and Enforceability Conditions

As noted above the developer had agreed to numerous measures. The inspector noted that:

> 'The likelihood of all the ... controls ... being observed in the longer term is in itself a factor in dealing with the issue of public confidence .... a number of the controls by conditions on day to day management of the site would ... be difficult to enforce in practice'.

The Inspector concluded as follows:

> 'The risk of larger dust emissions and of harmful effects .... cannot be wholly discounted where control is reliant on a complex range of ... measures ..., and medically based standards for dust concentrations are not available to assess risks objectively.'

The Secretary of State directed that the application be referred to him and found: *'The Secretary of State agrees with the Inspector that the incineration of chemical waste must be subject to stringent planning controls to overcome the environmental objections'* and also that *'planning permission should be conditional upon a chimney of an increased height from the existing one if liquid chemical waste is to be incinerated. It was also determined that other works are required on-site before such waste is processed, it would therefore not be appropriate to grant retrospective planning permission'.*

The Inspector found that previous operations at the site were poor and the question was whether significant improvements would make it acceptable.

It was determined that resumption of use of the plant for incineration of chemical waste would require compliance with conditions relating to:

- inspection, making good and clean-up of drum storage areas;
- soil sampling to assess contamination;
- results and programme for improvement of site;
- regrading and installation of surface water drainage system;
- provision of agreed drainage scheme and failsafe drainage channel;
- bunds of a construction approved by LPA;
- plan of the site to go to LPA;
- fitting of gas scrubbing;
- a chimney of 37m, with provision for monitoring;
- specification for scrubbers and chimney in accordance with BPM under; advice produced by HMIP;
- no incineration at weekends, except in an emergency; and
- plans for clean-up after operation;

The Inspector acknowledged that *'it would be unwise to allow such incineration and housing to be as close together as in Hucknall, but the courts have found it to be a lawful use of the land. It is in my view reasonable to make further allowance for these circumstances, and see if a reasonable balance can be struck which would enable the plant to operate while guaranteeing the improved amenity of the adjacent area'.*

He found he could not accept that waste licence conditions would ensure adequate plant conditions because these apply to a *particular operator* who cannot be refused a licence except on very limited grounds, therefore, there was a need to consider relatively onerous conditions which *'apply to any future operator and go with the land'.*

It was further stated that: *'We need an end to past land use problems, not merely power to act against a particular licence holder. The application site has to be put in order and necessary remedial action taken to remedy existing effects'.*

It appears that the waste management licence was considered to apply to a process only and that its provisions stop at ground level, therefore there was a need for planning conditions to safeguard the land.

It is apparent, therefore, that most conditions attached do *'go with the land'* and would not be available under the licence, which is for the operation and would not even be available under EPA Part 1 Authorisation which relates to the process. Two remaining conditions relate to requiring compliance with HMIP's BPM guidance.

C6.18   NONTOX LIMITED AND LANSTAR WASTE TREATMENT AGAINST A REFUSAL OF PLANNING PERMISSION BY HIGHLAND REGIONAL COUNCIL FOR AN INCINERATOR ON AN INDUSTRIAL ESTATE (APRIL 1990)

The Inspector was assisted at the appeal by a District Inspector from HMIP. The issues were determined and included the following:

- *'is the site suitable for any form of incineration process'*
- *'is the form of incineration now proposed, likely to cause unacceptable environmental effects'*
- *'is it possible for adequate controls to be imposed by means of conditions attached to:*

  (a)   *any disposal licence and/or authorisation issued by the WDA or HMIP;*

  (b)   *any planning permission that might be granted as a result of these appeals;*

- *'are alleged difficulties in relation to monitoring and control as severe as depicted by the two local authorities, and do they provide sufficient justification for refusing planning permission'.*

The Inspector stated that incineration would probably be regarded as BPEO rather than tankering material long distances to a suitable landfill.

Regarding the first issue it was stated that the height of the chimney had to be limited because of the proximity of an adjacent airport; and that this in turn would affect the material that is acceptable for incineration.

The Inspector considered that it was *'Clear that the site would be unsuitable for a full-scale incinerator, because of the need for sophisticated gas-scrubbing equipment and a stack of increased height, incompatible with the airport'.*

He did not consider the *'pattern of land uses in the vicinity to warrant refusal of planning permission for an incinerator at the appeal site, provided that adequate safeguards can be built in to ensure safe and satisfactory operating techniques and to minimise pollution risks'.*

On the third issue he stated "*Notwithstanding that the operation of the incinerator seems probable in future to fall under the control of HMIP. I am satisfied that adequate controls can be imposed by the relevant authorities which, if* adhered to, would ensure the maintenance of satisfactory environmental standards". Continuing that ... 'The vast majority of these matters will more appropriately be the concern of the WDA and/or HMIP, but I believe it was appropriate for them to be canvassed and debated at the planning stage as, if I had not been satisfied that satisfactory controls were capable of being imposed, that could have been a material consideration in my determination of these planning and enforcement appeals'.

Regarding the fourth issue the decision was that: 'Parliament has laid down the obligations of these bodies with regard to monitoring and control, and it cannot be right that a development proposal should not be allowed to proceed because it is alleged that the controlling agencies are unable to adequately meet these obligations'.

Finally, explaining the decision to grant the appeal it was stated that, 'my conclusions on these matters have been reached on the understanding that the vast majority of the matters of concern to the local authorities and the public are capable of control by the WDA and/or HMIPI'.

C6.19   FAYGLEN LIMITED AGAINST THE REFUSAL BY HERTFORDSHIRE COUNTY COUNCIL OF PLANNING PERMISSION FOR THE IMPORTATION OF INERT MATERIAL TO RESTORE A REFUSE-FILLED MINERAL WORKING AND FOR LANDSCAPING (MAY 1991)

The appeal was dismissed but it was noted that the Council had accepted that provisions in a draft Section 106 Agreement to monitor and control the production of landfill gas were sufficient to overcome their initial concern which led to the third reason for refusing the application.

C6.20   REDROW HOMES (NORTHERN) LIMITED AGAINST A REFUSAL BY STOCKPORT METROPOLITAN BOROUGH COUNCIL TO GRANT OUTLINE PLANNING PERMISSION FOR ERECTION OF NEIGHBOURHOOD CENTRE COMPRISING A LOCAL COMMUNITY FOOD STORE, PUBLIC HOUSE/RESTAURANT, CAR SHOWROOMS AND PETROL SALES (JULY 1991)

'The Inspector determined that 'provided full details of the protective measures relating to the construction of buildings and protection at its boundaries are the subject of an appropriate planning condition the means of dispersal of gas could be acceptable'. In fact the appeal was granted with the following as one of a number of conditions:

'Before any development commences on the site a scheme giving full details of appropriate gas protection measures proposed to prevent the penetration of landfill gas shall be submitted to and approved by the Local Planning Authority. Such a scheme shall include provision for the monitoring of the gas protection measures approved during the period of construction and after the completion of building works'.

Presumably, no other controls were available on the land and it is an acceptable condition because it is practicable, enforceable and does not conflict with other available controls.

C6.21   *FERRO ALLOYS AND METALS LIMITED AGAINST A REFUSAL BY HIGH PEAK BOROUGH COUNCIL TO GRANT PLANNING PERMISSION FOR RETENTION OF A CHIMNEY AND AGAINST AN ENFORCEMENT NOTICE REQUIRING REMOVAL OF THE CHIMNEY AS A CONDITION OF PLANNING PERMISSION (JULY 1989)*

The Inspector stated that although it was accepted that the process was the source of pollution and the chimney was the pollution control device, the chimney did influence what areas were affected by the emissions and that such emissions can be a material planning consideration. He considered that *'the Council are entitled to say (provided that they have the evidence), that the chimney has spread pollution in an unsatisfactory way and that permission should not be renewed'.*

He also added, however, that *'The effect of the removal of the chimney on the future of the factory, its production and its employees (ie closure) is of course a very material factor in reaching a decision on the planning merits.'*

The Appellants second objection to the second reason for refusal was that it was not the purview of the LPA to use planning conditions to achieve objectives that would be better under pollution control legislation.

The Inspector stated that because the Council genuinely considered that their wish for reduced emissions would not be achieved through the more specific powers of HMIP, the Council's approach was reasonable, given the evidence on HMIP's policy and the operators likely financial position.

This is in contrast to other decisions where the potential inability of HMIP to enforce controls was not grounds for refusal. The Inspector went on to state *'I do not consider, however, that refusal of planning permission can be justified on the assumption that the improvement notice will not be complied with.'*

Consequently the appeal was granted subject to the condition that:

'The emissions of Sulphur Dioxide from the chimney shall not at any time, after Monday 31 August 1992, exceed 113kg per hour'.

[It must be emphasised in this case that HMIP was operating under the old pollution control regime. Whether such a decision would have been necessary or justifiable under the new regime is not clear].

C6.22   *MONMOUTH BOROUGH COUNCIL AGAINST NON-DETERMINATION BY GWENT COUNTY COUNCIL FOR PLANNING PERMISSION FOR A LANDFILL SITE AT PWLLDU, BLAENAVON*

The application was submitted by Monmouth Borough Council (MBC) as WDA. The site straddled a National Park Boundary so it fell to be determined by GCC. Monmouth appealed against non-determination and the case was called in by SoSW and a public inquiry was held. The appeal was refused in a decision given in July 1990.

Much of the inquiry was taken up with examining the adequacy of the arrangements for leachate disposal including detailed consideration of hydrology and hydrogeology. GCC demonstrated that there was far less certainty about leachate and methane pathways than was claimed and that the proposal to tip the liquor down a disused mineshaft was potentially damaging and environmentally unacceptable.

Both the Inspector and SoSW considered that *"reduction and disposal of leachate is a fundamental issue in these appeals and ... planning permission should not be granted until all matters relating to the issue have been fully considered and satisfactorily resolved"*. It was therefore concluded that *"the proposals in their present form are incomplete and therefore are unacceptable"*. The appeal was refused.

In January 1991 MBC submitted a revised application for a containment rather than a 'dilute and disperse' site. The application was supported by an Environmental Statement in respect of which GCC requested more information. SoSW called in the application for his determination. GCC has asked that a full planning inquiry be held. No action has yet been signalled by SoSW.

C6.23   *ADDITIONAL CASE*

APPEAL AGAINST DECISION BY TRAFFORD BOROUGH COUNCIL TO REFUSE PLANNING PERMISSION FOR THE EXTENSION OF LANDFILLING FOLLOWED BY RESTORATION TO AMENITY/WOODLAND AT PEALES NOOK LANDFILL, MANCHESTER ROAD, TRAFFORD, MANCHESTER.

The inspector's main considerations were:

- Would the land be put to use as a motorcycle trail park, in accordance with a local plan proposal.

- In light of the conclusion to the first issue, whether the degree of conflict with the key local planning policies, and the harm to the objectives of these policies that would ensue from this would be outweighed by the additional contribution the extra tipping void would make towards meeting the waste disposal needs of Greater Manchester.

- Whether, bearing in mind need considerations, the modifications to the landform would be acceptable in their visual impact on the surrounding Mersey Valley area.

The inspector considered that, for a number of reasons, development of the sites as a motorcycle trail park in event that landfilling did not proceed, was unlikely and that consequently the weight accorded to this issue was diminished.

In examining the need for tipping space the inspector noted that the development would only satisfy about one year's tipping demand and that whilst alternative capacity undoubtedly existed although the Council had not identified any, its use if outside the Metropolitan boundary, would inevitably entail additional environmental and transport costs.

Examining the proposal against Local Plan policies the inspector found that there was no site specific need case, but noted the industrial character of the area as diminishing the effect on the valley character that would otherwise occur if the site were located elsewhere. The inspector states 'This is not, however, the same as contributing to the improvement of the Valley which (Policy) P1 requires if the need test is not satisfied'.

He goes on to state, however, that he does not consider that the 'objectives of the policies need be unduly prejudiced by the provision of additional tipping capacity in these predominantly industrial surrounding.'... providing an acceptable after-use is found.

It was the consideration of visual impact that determined the issue. the development as proposed would 'present an extensive, monolithic and excessively high, form'. He concluded that the proposal's 'visual impact would be severe and that it does not come close enough to improving the valley character as required by P1 to justify treating it as an exception to the general presumption of that policy against further tipping in the Valley, even though a degree of need exists.'

Annex D

Information Sources

PLANNING GUIDANCE

Department of the Environment (1984) *Planning Control Over Hazardous Developments* (Circular 9/84) HMSO London

Department of the Environment (1985) *Planning Conditions* (Circular 1/85) HMSO London

Department of the Environment (1985) *Planning Control Over Oil And Gas Operations* (Circular 2/85) HMSO London

Department of the Environment (1987) *Development of Contaminated Land* (Circular 21/87) HMSO London

Department of the Environment (1988) *Applications, Permissions And Conditions* (MPG 2) HMSO London

Department of the Environment (1988) *Environmental Assessment* (Circular 13/88) HMSO London

Department of the Environment (1988) *General Development Order* HMSO London

Department of the Environment (1989) *Environmental Assessment: A Guide to the Procedures.* HMSO London

Department of the Environment (1989) *Landfill Sites - Development Control* (Circular 17/89) HMSO London

Department of the Environment (1990) *Reclamation of Mineral Workings* (MPG 7) HMSO London

Department of the Environment (1991) *General Policy and Principles*, draft PPG 1, DoE London

Department of the Environment (1991) *Planning Obligations* (Circular 16/91) HMSO London

Department of the Environment (1991) *Planning and Noise*, draft PPG, DoE, London

Department of the Environment (1991) *Regional Planning Guidance for East Anglia* RPG6, HMSO, London.

Department of the Environment (1991) *Water Industry Investment*: Planning Considerations, (Circular 17/91), HMSO London

Department of the Environment (1992) *Development Plans and Regional Planning Guidance* (PPG 12) HMSO London

SERPLAN (1987) *Guidelines for Waste Disposal Planning in the South East* RPC 900 Serplan London

(English numbers only used in references to planning guidance).

OTHER GOVERNMENT AND AGENCY GUIDANCE

Department of the Environment (1989) *The Licensing of Waste Facilities, Waste Management* Paper No 4, HMSO London

Department of the Environment (1990) *This Common Inheritance - Britain's Environmental Strategy* HMSO London

Department of the Environment *The Licensing of Waste Disposal Sites, Waste Management* Paper No 4

Department of the Environment (1987) *Landfilling Wastes* (Waste Management Paper No 26) HMSO London

Department of the Environment and the Welsh Office *Integrated Pollution Control - A Practical Guide* (undated)

Department of the Environment, Scottish Office, Welsh Office (1991) *Secretary of State's Guidance (Processes Prescribed for Air Pollution Control by Local Authorities)*, HMSO London

GG1 (91)	*Introduction to Part I of the Act*
GG2 (91)	*Authorisations*
GG3 (91)	*Applications and Registers*

HMIP *Determination of Authorisations* (Internal Guidance Note) (undated)

HMIP *Guidance Note to Applicants for Authorisation - Processes Prescribed for Regulation by Her Majesty's Inspectorate of Pollution* (undated)

National Rivers Authority (1991) *Policy and Practice for the Protection of Groundwater. Draft for Consultation* NRA, Solihull

NRA Thames Region (1991) *Town & Country Planning Liaison Procedures*

KEY REFERENCES FROM PUBLISHED LITERATURE

Ball, S and Bell, S (1991) *Environmental Law*, Blackstone, London

Bettle, J (1988) Noise: Problems of Overlapping Controls in *Journal of Planning and Environmental Law*, May pp 323-330

Cross D T., Guruswamy, LD, Pearce, BJ and Tromans, SR (1988) *BPEO through the planning System*, University of Cambridge, Clare Hall Pollution Research Group, Cambridge

Crossthwaite, PJ and Bichard, E M (1990) Risk Assessment - A Tool for Planners, in *The Planner* Vol 76 (9) March 9th, pp 9-10

East Midlands Regional Planing Forum (1991) *Regional Strategy for the East Midlands: Consultation Draft*

Gibbs, K (1991) Recent Legislation for Environmental Protection in *The Planner* Vol 77 (33) September

Hawke, N. and Himan, J (1988) Water Pollution: Plugging the Leaks, in *Journal of Planning and Environment Law*, October pp 670-673

Miller, C (1988) Planning, Pollution and Hazard, in *Urban Law and Policy* Vol. 9pp 83-108

Miller, C (1990) Development Control as in instrument of environmental management in *Town Planning Review* Vol 61 (3) pp 231-245

Miller, C and Wood, C (1983) *Planning and Pollution*, Clarendon, Oxford

Pugh Smith, J (1992) *The Local Authority as a Regulator of Pollution in the 1990s* in Journal of Planning and Environmental Law

Raemaekers, J, Cowie, L, and Wilson, E (1991) An Index of Local Authority Green Plans. Research Paper No 37. Edinburgh College of Art/Heriot Watt University

Shelbourn, C (1989) Development Control and Hazardous Substances, in *Journal of Planning and Environment Law*, May pp 323-330

Shelbourn, C (1991) Are We Doing Enough? in *New Law Journal* Vol. 141 (6528) November 15, pp 1562-1565

South West Regional Planning Conference (1991) *Towards a Regional Strategy*

Tromans, S. and Clarkson, M (1991). The Environmental Protection Act 1990: Its Relevance to Planning Controls, in *Journal of Planning and Environmental Law*, June, pp 507-515

Walker, G (1991) Land Use Planning and Industrial Hazards, A Role for the European Community, in *Land Use Policy* Vol. 8 (3) July, pp 227-240

West Midlands Regional Forum of Local Authorities (1991) *The West Midlands: Your Region, Your Future* WMRF, Stratford

Wood, C (1986). Local Planning Authority Controls over Pollution, in *Policy and Politics* Vol 14 (1), pp 107-123

Wood, C (1988) *Planning Pollution Prevention* Heinemann, London

Wood, C and Hooper, P (1989) The effects of the relaxation of planning controls in enterprise zones on industrial pollution in *Environment and Planning* A Vol 21 (9) pp 1157-67

D2.1   *Local Planning Authorities Interviewed in Connection with the Research*

County Councils

Avon
Cheshire
Clwyd
Durham
Gwent
Hampshire
Kent
Leicestershire

District Councils

Delyn
Easington
Ellesmere Port and Neston
Glanford
New Forest
North Warwickshire
Torfaen

Unitary Bodies

Doncaster
Gateshead
Sandwell with Black Country Development Corporation
Wirral

D2.2   *Interview Protocol*

The following protocol was used as a basis for interviews carried out with LPAs.

Development Planning

(1) *Context*

- Role of Interviewee

- Structure of LPA: who is responsible for pollution and waste control and the formulation of policy on these issues?

(2) *Current Development Plans*

- Which development plans are currently used?

- Are there any policies which specifically address pollution/waste control issues?

- Are there any general/indirect/good intention policies?

- Do any policies directly/indirectly tackle the issue of "bad neighbour" development?

- Are any of the policies set out in the waste development plan reiterated in development plans, and vice versa?

- And Minerals subject plans?

(3) *Consultation of Existing Plans*

- Which consultees provided inputs to the preparation of the existing development plans (eg, HMIP, NRA, WRA)?

- At which stage of plan preparation did consultation take place?

- How useful were inputs from consultees in forming policies on waste/pollution control?

- In the case of unitary authorities, were there any differences in the scope and nature of consultations for UDPs compared to Structure and Local Plans.

(4) *Development Control*

- Which source/types of information does the planning authority generally draw upon when dealing with the pollution or waste implications of a development proposal?

- How useful are Environmental Statements in aiding the decision-making process?

- How useful is consultation with pollution, waste and advisory authorities prior to determination of applications?

- To what extent do matters regulated by other authorities form material considerations in the determination of planning applications?

- Does the planning authority ever impose planning conditions to consents to control pollution or waste (potential for overlap or conflict with other waste provisions)?

- Does the planning authority impose planning conditions in the management of waste disposal sites in addition to conditions on waste management licences (eg, for restoration of the site)?

- What actions does the planning authority generally take to control or manage landfill sites in the post-closure phase?

- If appropriate, are there any differences in the way the planning authority considers pollution and waste issues in Enterprise Zones or Simplified Planning Zones as compared with other areas?

D3.1   STRUCTURE PLANS

Clwyd County Structure Plan first Alteration Submitted Written Statement and Explanatory Memorandum, January 1990

Cornwall Structure Plan incorporating the First Alteration Approved by the Secretary of State, March 1991

Durham County Structure Plan. Approved Structure Plan Policies incorporating Alteration No. 1 and Alteration No. 3, 1989
(note: Alteration No. 3 approved August 1990)

Dyfed Structure Plan (including Alteration No.1) Approved by the Secretary of State for Wales, November 1990

Kent Planning Strategy for Kent. Approved Kent Structure Plan and Explanatory Memorandum, 1990

Lancashire Structure Plan Written Statement. Approved by the Secretary of State, March 1991

Leicestershire Structure Plan. Submission Draft Explanatory Memorandum, November 1991

Norfolk to 2006 - Structure Plan Review Consultation Draft, July 1990

North Yorkshire County Structure Plan. Amended by Alterations Nos. 1 and 2, approved by the Secretary of State, January 1990

Nottinghamshire County Structure Plan Replacement Approved with modifications by the Secretary of State, September 1991

Warwickshire Structure Plan Alterations 1989-2001 Consultation Draft, January 1990
(note: the Plan was approved with modifications in 1991)

D3.2   UNITARY DEVELOPMENT PLANS

Bexley Unitary Development Plan. Consultation Draft, September 1991

Coventry Into the 21st Century - City of Coventry Unitary Development Plan. Approved by Coventry City Council for Public Deposit, February 1991

Newcastle upon Tyne Draft Unitary Development Plan, May 1991

Sheffield A City for People. The Draft Unitary Development Plan, February 1991

Tower Hamlets Draft Unitary Development Plan. Consultation Draft, August 1991

Wakefield Metropolitan District Unitary Development Plan. Revised Draft Plan. Reasoned Policy Justification Volume 2, October 1991

Wigan Unitary Development Plan. Consultation Draft Written Statement, November 1991

D3.3   *LOCAL PLANS*

Copeland Local Plan. Draft Proposals, October 1991

Crawley Borough Local Plan. Deposit Draft, October 1990

Erewash Borough Local Plan. Draft Written Statement, December 1990

Forest Heath Local Plan. Public Consultation Draft, August 1990

Glanford: West Glanford Local Plan. Adopted Plan (as modified), 1989

Mid Bedfordshire Local Plan. Deposit Copy and Proposed Changes, July 1989 - April 1991

South Staffordshire Local Plan. Draft for Consultation, September 1991

Torfaen The Local Plan. Draft Written Statement, July 1991

Warrington Borough Local Plan. Consultation Draft, April 1990

Woodspring: Clevedon, Nailsea and Portishead Area Local Plan Deposit Version, 1990

Department of the Environment

Waste Management Division	:	Mr J Rouse
	:	Mr D Clare
	:	Mr M Burn
Waste Technical Division	:	Mr K Pearce
Air Quality Division	:	Mr M Etkind
	:	Mr S Bland
Water WRE2	:	Mr D Pearson
Minerals	:	Mrs A Ward
IPC Policy	:	Mr I Pickard

The Welsh Office

Planning Department	:	Mr C Morgan

The Planning Inspectorate

	:	Mr I James
	:	Mr C Jenkins

Her Majesty's Inspectorate of Pollution

	:	Mr T Lennon
	:	Mr S Yardley

National Rivers' Authority

	:	Mr R Evans

Confederation of British Industry

	:	Mr T Thairs

NAWDC

	:	Mr S Webb